SURVIVAL SKILLS OF THE NATIVE AMERICANS

SURVIVAL SKILLS OF THE NATIVE AMERICANS

Hunting, Trapping, Woodwork, and More

Edited by
STEPHEN BRENNAN

Skyhorse Publishing

Skyhorse Publishing books may be purchased in bulk at special discounts for sales promotion, corporate gifts, fund-raising, or educational purposes. Special editions can also be created to specifications. For details, contact the Special Sales Department, Skyhorse Publishing, 307 West 36th Street, 11th Floor, New York, NY 10018 or info@skyhorsepublishing.com.

Skyhorse® and Skyhorse Publishing® are registered trademarks of Skyhorse Publishing, Inc.®, a Delaware corporation.

Visit our website at www.skyhorsepublishing.com.

10 9 8 7 6 5 4 3

Library of Congress Cataloging-in-Publication Data is available on file.

Cover design by Tom Lau
Cover photos: iStockphoto

Print ISBN: 978-1-63220-717-3
Ebook ISBN: 978-1-63220-865-1

Printed in China

TABLE OF CONTENTS

NOTE

We err when we regard *survival skills* purely in terms of the response to an immediate extreme danger or situation—an enemy lurking behind the tree over there, a grizzly surprised at play with her young, a freak late summer blizzard, or famine when the buffalo do not come. Properly understood, survival skills also embrace the means by which whole cultures developed and endured.

Our survey of the survival skills of the Native Americans is by no means exhaustive, which would be impossible. At the time of the European Contact it's estimated that there were something like twelve hundred distinct peoples inhabiting the Americas, each with its own language, customs, material culture, and other imperatives associated with climatic and other challenges of each particular region.

Therefore we have limited our scope to the peoples of North America, and we have largely—except in the case of the horse—confined our survey to Native American ways and culture before Contact. Our strategy has been to sample the challenges, cultures, and techniques of specific peoples, and to allow them to stand in for and to illustrate survival skills of Native Americans generally.

This book employs the various terms *Native Americans, Indians,* and *First Peoples* interchangeably—with respect and without prejudice—recognizing that people most often associate and identify themselves with a specific local, familial, or cultural group; so whenever possible we've identified the artifacts, customs, and skills in our sampling with particular regional and tribal peoples.

CHAPTER ONE: TOOL KITS

For the thousands of years before Contact, the Native American peoples employed a *lithic*, or stone-age tool kit, comprised of stone, wood, shell, horn, bone, and plant and animal fiber.

But stone was the key, the one resource whose use made not only all the myriad things of daily life but also the tools from which other materials might be shaped and fashioned. This shaping process, the means by which stone was made to assume artificial forms adapted to human needs, was varied and ingenious, and its mastery was a matter of the greatest importance to Native American peoples.

SHAPING STONE

The primary tool was the hammerstone. This might be of any size or weight—depending on the task to

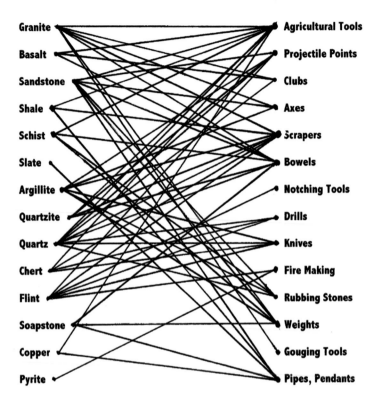

Granite	Agricultural Tools
Basalt	Projectile Points
Sandstone	Clubs
Shale	Axes
Schist	Scrapers
Slate	Bowels
Argillite	Notching Tools
Quartzite	Drills
Quartz	Knives
Chert	Fire Making
Flint	Rubbing Stones
Soapstone	Weights
Copper	Gouging Tools
Pyrite	Pipes, Pendants

be undertaken—but it needed to be hard, relatively smooth, and able to be held in the hand. Quartzite makes a fine hammerstone because of its density and because it cannot be easily split. Water-worn stones, found by the sea or lakeshores and in stream

beds, provided convenient tools for breaking, driving, grinding, and cracking.

Hammerstones

Simple tools did not need to be elaborate, and they could be made at once with a few blows of the hammerstone; many hammers, axes, knives, picks, scrapers, and the like were made with ease. But the more highly specialized implements, tools, and weapons required considerable time and effort.

The first step was to locate the proper stone (or to trade for it) and then rough out the material from

which the implements were to be fashioned. This involved fracturing the stone into the *blanks*, which were to be worked. This initial process was done with a hammerstone of one size or another. If the core was large, a large hammerstone might be wielded in two hands, or it might even be thrown.

PERCUSSION AND PRESSURE FRACTURING

Once the craftsman had assembled several likely blanks, he continued to work the stone using a combination of *percussion* and *pressure* fracturing techniques until he had fashioned the desired blade or implement.

A percussion fracture is accomplished by striking the blank a glancing blow with a hammerstone held in the hand, or by means of stick, a hafted stone, or an antler.

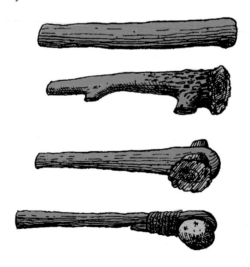

Pressure fracturing is the technique by which the arrow-point, blade, or other implement is completed, and involves the application of pressure to the edge of the stone being worked.

Most often an antler was the tool of choice. The craftsman might hold the stone in his hand, or he might work it on a stone or wooden *anvil*.

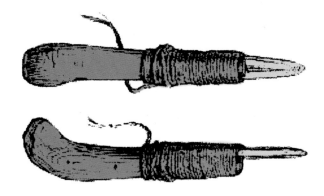

ARROW REPAIR

On the war path or hunt, the warrior might find it necessary to repair his arrow, in which case this repair tool of wood and antler would come in handy to both sharpen and straighten his arrow.

PECKING

Another technique for working stone is known as *pecking* or *crumbling*. The action is percussive and results in the crumbling of minute portions of the surface of the stone, which disappear as dust. Besides striking implements such as axes, clubs, and hammers, pecking was also used in the shaping of the stone mortar and pestle, stone pots, figurines, and other stone images. Pecking was also commonly used in finishing arrowheads and other bladed tools, as well as for close work like shaping stone drill bits.

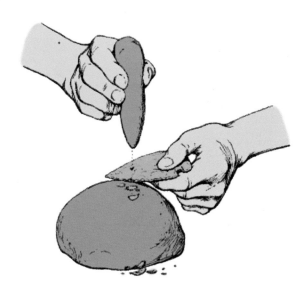

MAKING A STONE AX

Pecking an Ax Head

Use a hammerstone weighing something under a pound. A larger stone is not necessarily better, as you will tire more quickly. Choose one that you can easily hold between your thumb and fingertips—perhaps a rounded pebble from a beach or water course. With this you will also find that you can comfortably change your grip to offer a new surface when it has worn away.

For the ax head you will need to choose a stone roughly the size and shape of the intended finished ax and ideally of a slightly softer stone.

Hold the ax-head-to-be in one hand and the hammerstone in the other, and rapidly strike the surface you wish to shape. Held like this in the hand, the ax head is easily turned to meet the blows of the hammer, and the elasticity of the hand support prevents breakage under strokes—were the ax head stationary, it would shatter. Be sure to hold or support the ax head stone under the point of percussion.

Choose an easy rhythm, striking neither too hard nor too gently. Swing the hammerstone from your wrist and elbow so that it bounces slightly back after

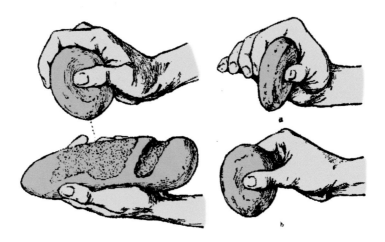

each successive blow. Each strike should be roughly at a right angle to the surface you are working. Be patient.

If you intend to haft your ax, you will need to groove your stone. This will require a hammerstone with a pointed end—rather egg-shaped—no wider than the planned groove. You will find that you need to replace this stone more often. Your goal is to create a U-shaped groove, though not so deep that you threaten the integrity of the ax head. The depth of the groove is determined by the width of the handle you plan to use.

Polishing the Ax Head

A pecked ax head will never give you a really sharp cutting tool. A stone ax doesn't cut per se; rather its action is to bruise and to break. But you can get a better edge on your stone by a process of *abrasion,* or *polishing.* For this you will need a slab of sedimentary rock—sandstone is best—and water. Rub the ax head energetically back and forth across the surface of rock, taking care to keep it well watered. This creates a slurry of grit and water that facilitates the polishing. It will probably take an hour of hard work, but be patient. For a utility ax, only the edge needs this treatment. If you wish to remove the pecking marks from the whole ax head, you will need to find a rock with concave indentations that roughly approximate the convex features of your ax. When you are satisfied, wash thoroughly and dry, once or twice, and lightly grease or oil the ax head.

Hafting the Ax Head

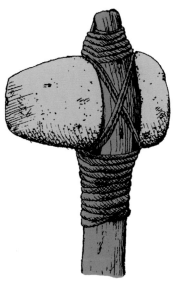

The three methods most often used in hafting the stone ax:

For the ax handle, choose a straight, dense, hardwood branch, forked at one end, of roughly the right shape to snugly seat the ax handle. Tie it tightly off with well-wetted rawhide.

If the ax handle has no natural fork, split the wood at one end and wedge the stone there. Tie it off as above.

Alternatively, choose an ax handle that is ten inches or so longer than the intended length of your tool. Cut away enough of the shaft to a depth roughly conforming to the configuration of the groove in the ax head.

Boil or steam the wood until it is soft enough to work, then slowly bend the wood into the grooves and around the head. Lash the wrapped end to the body of the handle. Take your time. The wood will have to be heated multiple times and patiently worked.

CORDAGE

The Native peoples of North America made use of everything their environment had to offer, and plant and animal fiber was central to their material culture. This fiber was everywhere, and they were quick to learn which of the many plants was best for their intended purposes.

Small Plant Fibers

After harvesting the stalks to be used, break off the roots and the very top of the plant. If the stalk has dried, break it along its length and strip out the fibers from the top end of the stalk, branch, or limb, working down toward its base. Take care not to break the fiber around the nodes of the plant. The most useful fibers are found between the skin or sheath of the plant and the inner pith, but this plant "skin" was also very useful for lashing and for basketry.

Clean the plant fibers as you go, stripping out any adhering impurities. You don't want to work with fibers that are too dry or brittle, so you may wish to dampen them.

Bark Fibers

Tree bark was also an important source of fiber for the Native North American peoples. The choice of bark for fiber depended on what was available, but basswood was often used. This tree offered long, strong, supple fibers and was found throughout North America.

The basswood fibers are harvested (most easily in the spring) by stripping the bark from the tree limb. With a little work with finger and thumb, this bark will separate into an outer and an inner layer. It is the fiber from the inner layer that is the most useful for cordage (though, again, the Native peoples used the outer layer for mats, baskets, and lashings).

Tree bark was often boiled for a day or two in a mixture of water and ash to remove the sap adhering to the fibers.

Once the fibers have been stripped out and cleaned, they are ready for cording as below.

Sinew

Sinew from leg tendons and the backstrap of North American mammals—deer, elk, bighorn mountain sheep, moose, bear, and buffalo—provided a lot of fibers. The sinew was harvested when the animals were butchered. It was then dried for later cording.

Dried tendons are prepared by hammering the tendon along its length, dampening the fibers, and stripping out the excess matter.

Fiber from the backstrap is obtained by manipulating the dried backstrap, breaking the membrane until it is supple, dampening it, then separating the fibers from the impurities.

Cording

Once you have a sufficient number of fibers for the thread or rope you wish to cord, hold a bunch of fiber in the middle by the thumb and index finger of your left hand. You should have top and bottom bundles of strands and the two bundles should be roughly equal in length and volume.

Working from this center, pinch about an inch-length of strands from the top bundle of fibers with the fingers of your right hand, twist them *to the right*, and pull them tight.

Then twist the fibers of the bottom bundle *to the left*, tightly, under and all the way around the top bundle. Advance the finger of your left hand to stabilize your work. The top bundle is now the bottom bundle, and the bottom is the top. Repeat this process until it is time to splice new fibers into the cord.

Splicing

Well before the fibers of either bundle have begun to thin out, lay another several fibers into the V between two bundles, bringing them out along the top bundle. Repeat the process above until it is time to splice in more fibers. The strongest cord is the cord most often spliced. The tighter you twist the fibers, the stronger the cordage.

The Leg-Roll

Another, and much faster, cording technique is the leg-roll method. Prepare the fibers as above.

Bend the batch into two bundles and lay them on your leg, just above your knee. Hold the batch of fibers in the middle with your left hand, then roll each of the bundles tightly with an outward motion of your right hand until they begin to kink. You now have two tightly rolled strands of several threads. Now roll these two

strands *together* until they also begin to kink. Hold this newly rolled cord in place with your right hand, and twist them together with the fingers of your left hand.

Rawhide

Rawhide thongs were cut from animal hide by lodging the cutting blade firmly in the ground and, working from the perimeter, pulling the hide against the edge of the blade. By this method a thong of any length and thickness could be cut. This was most often a two-person job, but the illustration gives a good idea of the technique involved. Afterward, the thongs were straightened by hand or by wetting and hanging them with weights.

The thongs were often braided rather than corded (as above with plant fiber and sinew) to make a more robust line.

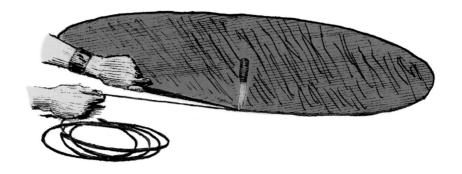

DRILLS

For the Native Americans before Contact, drill bits were of two distinct types: the solid and the tubular. The solid points might be made of any sharp or pointed stone, or other softer material—mineral, animal, or vegetable—and utilized sand as the abrading agent. The tubular forms may be of copper, bone, or wood, and also employed sand as the abrading agent. Joints of cane and the hollow bones of birds were often used. Tubular drills were generally used in boring hard materials like stone as well as softer materials.

The simplest form of an un-hafted rotary drill is the pointed stone held between the thumb and fingertips

and twirled back and forth; another is an implement of stone held in the hand and twirled back and forth with pressure, producing the desired bore.

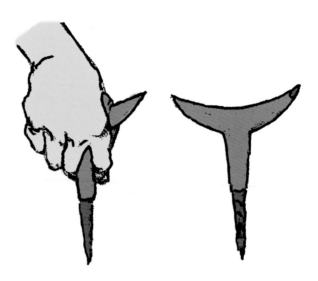

The ordinary way to use the shafted revolving drill was to rotate it back and forth between the palms of the hands, after the manner of the fire drill, or between one palm and the thigh. These methods were in common use throughout America.

Other devices for revolving the drill have been found in use by Native peoples. These implements are known as the pump, strap, bow, and disk drills.

Pump Drill

The pump drill consists of a shaft, which passes through a disk of stone, pottery, or wood, and a crosspiece through the pump drill; the shaft also runs through this crosspiece.

To each end of the crosspiece is attached a cord or thong, having sufficient play to allow it to pass over the top of the shaft and permitting the crosspiece to reach close to the disk. In setting the device in motion, the disk is turned to wind the string around the shaft. This raises the crosspiece. By pressing down quickly on the crosspiece, the wrapped end of the string unwinds, the shaft revolves, and the disk acquires sufficient momentum to rewind the string the moment the pressure on the crosspiece is removed.

By successive pressure and release, the reciprocal movement is kept up. The speed attained by this drill is much greater than that of the bow or the strap drill,

and it has the advantage of leaving one hand free to hold the object to be drilled.

Strap Drill

The strap drill was in use among the Eskimo and Aleuts in early—possibly pre-Columbian—times. The shaft here is kept in position by means of a headpiece of wood, which was held between the teeth. A strap or thong is wound once around the shaft, with one end being held in each hand, and is pulled alternately to the right and left, revolving the shaft. The thong was sometimes furnished with a handpiece of wood or bone at each end to allow a firmer grip. The chief advantage of this was that pressure could be regulated by pressure of the teeth on the mouthpiece. In some regions, instead of the mouthpiece, the top of the shaft was held by an assistant, and as much pressure was applied as necessary.

Bow Drill

The bow drill is closely related to the strap drill. The headpiece is held in position with one hand, while the strap bow drill is attached to the two ends of the bow and wrapped around the shaft. It is revolved by a backward and forward movement of the bow held in the other hand.

Disk Drill

The disk drill is a variant of the pump drill. The fixed disk of the pump drill is omitted, and a wide, movable disk takes the place of the movable crosspiece. Thongs are passed and attached through holes in opposite margins of the disk, one end to the top of the shaft and the other to the base near the drill point. The revolving motion is started by turning the disk until the thongs are twisted around the shaft and become taut.

When the disk is released and pressed suddenly downward, the strands unwind, revolving around the shaft, and the momentum winds them taut the other way. Sudden removal of the pressure on the disk causes the unwinding of the strands below, twirling the shaft in the opposite direction. By quick repetition of these movements, the motion is kept up and the work goes steadily on.

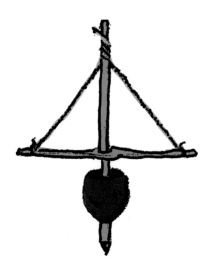

Weighted Drill

A weight was often added to the bit end of the drill. A couple of stones tied off to the shaft usually did the trick. This innovation not only provided extra downward force on the bit, it also added centrifugal force to the spinning shaft, acting much like a flywheel.

Starting a Fire by the Bow Drill Method

To get wood into the proper condition for starting a fire by the friction method requires, first, the selection of the proper kind of wood and, second, a thorough drying for weeks or even months. The wood must be as dry as wood can be made. Only certain kinds of woods, particularly cedar, balsam, and cottonwood, are really good for this purpose. The spindle and block must be of the same kind of wood and equally dry.

The materials needed are the bow, spindle, block, and tinder; you also need a shell, a stone with a small cavity, or another similar object that can be used as a bearing or cap on top of the spindle. A mussel shell was often used for the purpose, as it is light and has a hollow side that is smooth and makes an excellent bearing for the spindle end.

The bow, about two feet long, may be made of hickory or any springy wood, strung with stout, hard-laid twine.

The spindle, of any of the favorite woods, should be about sixteen inches long by three-fourths to one inch thick. The top should be rounded and the lower end should be shaped to a blunt, smooth point. *It must be very dry*.

The block should be an inch or a little more in thickness but of any convenient width and length that is still large enough to be easily held down firmly with the knees when working the drill in the kneeling position. It really ought be of the same kind of wood as the spindle.

The tinder, or *punk,* may be any inflammable material that can easily be fired from the burning dust, such as the shredded inner tree bark, very dry and fine, mixed with shredded dry leaves.

The operator cuts a V-shaped notch about three-quarters of an inch deep in the edge of the block. On the flat side of the block at the apex of the notch he then makes a small hole with the point of a knife as a starting place for the spindle.

Around this notch he places a small quantity of the tinder.

Then, giving the string of the bow a turn around the spindle, he kneels on the block, places the point of the spindle on the mark at the point of the notch, places the shell over the other end, and, throwing his weight upon the spindle, works the bow back and forth quickly and steadily.

The spindle, revolving rapidly, bores its way down into the block; the dust that is worn from the block

and spindle filters down through the notch among the dry tinder. An increasing heat develops from the friction of the dry wood, and soon an odor of scorching wood will be noticed; then a thin wisp of smoke arises from the dust in the notch and this grows stronger. After a while the smoldering fire itself is visible in the dust, which has accumulated in the notch and about the base of the spindle.

Here he stops the drill and blows the fire into flame, then places fine, dry twigs over the tinder; finally, he adds the coarser wood.

THE GREAT BURNS

For years American anthropologists and ethnologists have insisted that fire played no significant part in the shaping of the landscape by Native Americans. But recent studies, a wealth of accounts by the first European settlers, and the lore and traditions of the Native peoples themselves make it abundantly clear that fire was used extensively in managing the environment.

After harvesting their crops they frequently burned away the stubble, adding vital nitrates to the soil and setting up their fields for the next year's planting. Forests were cleared of underbrush, making for healthy stands of selected trees, and encouraging—and discouraging—the growth of particular varieties of plants. On the Great Plains they fired the grasslands in order to bring forth the sweet new buds so favored by the buffalo. This was particularly important to people who depended on drawing the herds to them in the times before the introduction of the horse.

Flint and Steel as Fire Starter

To strike a fire with flint, one must have some form of iron, and, while stone containing pyrites was used by some Eskimo and other tribes of the far north, it seems to have been unknown on the plains. Naturally, flint and steel were among the first articles introduced by white traders.

By striking glancing blows with a steel object along the edge of a piece of flint, showers of sparks were thrown into a little pile of tinder to be blown into a flame by the fire-kindler. It is said that for an expert the trick was not at all difficult, and that fire could be produced very quickly; but it is obvious that very dry materials were necessary.

BONE AND HORN TOOLS

(a) An antler scoop or prong, perhaps used for opening oysters
(b) An antler tool for working stone
(c) A bone projectile point
(d) A beaver tooth set in horn handle, used as a cutting tool

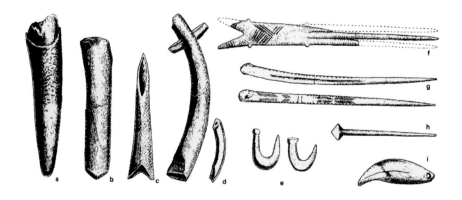

(e) Bone fishhooks
(f) Antler ornamental comb
(g) A bone needle or bodkin
(h) An antler pin, probably for fastening a garment
(i) A bear-tooth pendant

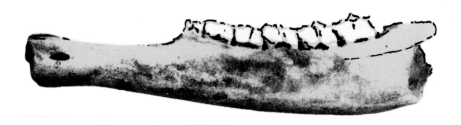

Another bone implement widely employed among eastern North American peoples was a piece of deer jaw used for scraping kernels from ears of corn.

CHAPTER TWO: WEAPONS: TOOLS FOR HUNTING AND WAR

Food supply and defense against enemies depended on the warrior's weapons. These were his most precious possessions, and he gave much care to their manufacture and maintenance.

Every weapon and every tool consists of two parts— that which cuts, wounds, or kills, and that by which it is held or worked.

Generally speaking, all weapons used by the Native peoples of the Americas, whether employed in warfare or in hunting, can be divided into three groups:

Weapons held and used in the hand for slashing, tearing, and piercing, such as stone and bone daggers, and micro-bladed wooden and bone swords.

KNIVES AND BLADES

A knife is only a hafted blade, which was commonly of worked bone, antler, or stone. If of stone, it was shaped

much as were the stone tools in the previous chapter, by process of percussion and pressure flaking, pecking, grinding, and polishing.

If of antler, the blade was shaped by cutting with a stone blade and then ground to achieve its point and edges. Bone blades were sometimes dried and split, before grinding as above.

Or weapons worked by some apparatus between the hand and the business end, like spears, lances, war clubs, hatchets, and tomahawks.

WAR CLUBS

A club is among the most fundamental of weapons, made for close-in combat, and is an extension and force-multiplier of the fist. Its function is to bruise, to stun, and to beat an enemy into submission. The practice of captive-taking played a important role in many Native American war cultures, and for this, it was the perfect tool.

A war club might be of any size and weight, but most often it conformed to the size of the warrior's forearm—weighted at the business end. The best war clubs were exquisitely balanced, with a slight curve to the arm, and made of hard, dense wood. Perhaps due to its ancient provenance, the war club was often a symbol of leadership and conveyed an aura of strength and prowess.

HATCHETS AND TOMAHAWKS

Often used interchangeably, hatchets and tomahawks differentiate in that a hatchet more correctly refers to a tool for cutting and chopping, while a tomahawk is a weapon of war. For the Native American warrior before Contact—and before steel became available for trade—the head of the weapon might be of stone, bone, or antler. Like the war club, it was a weapon that was used in close combat, and like the war club, it achieved a kind of symbolic status. When a people were decided on war, they were said to take up the tomahawk.

Or weapons thrown from the hand, like throwing sticks and bolas, or projectiles, like sling stones, arrows, harpoons, blow-tube darts, and the atlatl.

THROWING STICK

A hunting tool, sometimes called a "rabbit stick," the throwing stick somewhat resembles the boomerang—but it doesn't return to the thrower. Made of a single piece of slightly curved wood, the trick was to throw it with a flick of the wrist, so as to spin it. It is this spinning action that stuns or disables the rabbit or other game.

BOLA

The bola was made of two braided leather thongs, joined together and weighted at their ends with rounded stones. Used more often for hunting, it brought an animal down by wrapping around its legs.

SLING

The sling was used on the California coast north of San Francisco and in the southwestern regions of the Continent. It was most often fashioned of two loops of braided leather, with a patch of hide where the loops joined— for seating the projectile, which was usually a rounded, smooth stone. The sling was swung in a sidewise, windmill movement to build up energy. The trick was to let go of one loop at the moment of throwing. A practiced slinger could achieve wonderful accuracy.

BLOW TUBE AND DART

The blow tube was used in those areas where cane grew in abundance, especially in the southern areas of the Continent. The Muskhogean tribes and the Cherokees employed this weapon for killing birds in swamplands. The cane was split lengthwise, which allowed the inner material to be scraped away, then reassembled with glue or resin.

The peoples of the Gulf Coast made a compound blow tube by fastening four or five reeds together, although this version of the weapon was most common in Mexico and Central America.

The dart was a slight shaft of wood, almost the length of the tube, just a little thinner than the circumference of the hollow of the tube, and densely feathered at its back end. When the hunter spied his prey, he blew sharply into the tube, propelling the dart.

ATLATL—SPEAR THROWER

According to the archeological record, the atlatl was used throughout the far north, in southeastern Alaska, and on the coast of California and in Mexico. But it must also have played an important role in the hunting lives of North American Paleo-Indians.

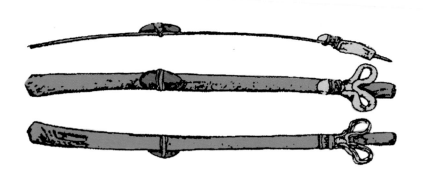

An arm extender, the Atlatl is a device for throwing a spear or dart with more force than capable of an arm alone. It consists of a baton about two feet in length, notched to fit into the butt of the spear and weighted to give it more force.

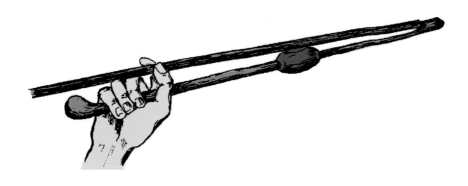

BOWS

In North America the universal projecting device for propelling arrows and barbed harpoons was the bow. It was found in its simplest form in the south and east and became more complicated to the westward and northward. Generally they are of the following types:

The ordinary or "self" bow was made of a single piece of hard, elastic wood.

The compound bow was made of two or more pieces of wood, whalebone, antler, horn, or bone fastened together.

The sinew-backed bow consisted of a single piece of yew or other wood, on the back of which shredded sinew was glued.

Peoples of the far north used sinew-corded bows almost exclusively. They were made from drift and other wood and are backed with finely twisted or braided sinew cord and reinforced with wedges, splints, and bridges.

Features of the Bow

Back, or part of the bow away from the archer.
Belly, or part toward the archer.

Limbs, or parts above and below the grip. Also called arms.

Grip, or portion held in the hand.

Nocks, or ends upon which the bowstring is attached.

Horns, or parts projecting beyond the limbs. At the end are the nocks.

String, made of sinew or cord.

Seizing, the application of string to prevent the splitting of the wood.

Backing, sinew or other substance laid on to increase the elasticity.

Wrist guard, any device used to prevent the bowstring from wounding the wrist of the hand holding the bow.

Bow Woods

Mexican border: Cottonwood, willow, mezquit, bois d'arc, juniper.

Southern United States: Hickory, oak, ash, hornbeam, walnut.

Northeastern United States: Hickory, oak, ash, walnut, hornbeam, sycamore, dogwood, and, indeed, any of the many species of hard wood.

Mississippi Valley: Same as on the Atlantic slope.

Plains: Bois d'arc, coffee tree, ash, and wood procured in trade.

Interior basin: Mezquit in the south, abundant woods in the north, hard and elastic, of many species.

California and Oregon: Evergreen woods, yew, spruce.

Columbia River: Same as California.

Southeastern Alaska: Willow, spruce.

Western Canada: Birch, willow, maple, spruce, cedar.

Eskimo: Driftwood and timber from whale ships and wrecks.

Types of Bows

Bow staves were kept on hand in different stages of readiness in every lodge or wigwam. The Native American was always on the lookout for a good piece of wood or other raw material. This, he or she thought, will make a good snowshoe frame or bow or arrow and I will cut it down. These began to be worked at once, bent, straightened, steamed, scraped, and shaped. Young men took pains to acquire and practice these arts. When they became old, and could no longer take the field, they found a place among their people as a bowyer.

The design of the bow depended on the materials available in each given region.

The *hard-wood self-bow* was used in all of North America east of the Rocky Mountains and south of Hudson Bay. This area extended beyond the mountains along the southern border; and even in places where the compound bow was also used, it remained the fundamental pattern.

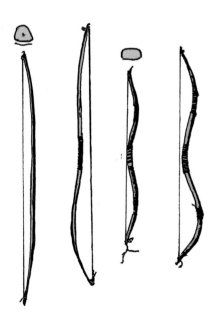

The *compound bow* is one in which the grip and the two wings are separate pieces. There are two compound-bow areas, the Northeast Inuit and the Sioux. The compound bows of the Sioux were made of buffalo and sheep horn and of the elk antler. In both types the compound bow arose from a scarcity of wood for making a self-bow.

The *sinew-lined bow* is one in which finely shredded sinew is mixed with glue and laid on so that it resembles bark. This bow was used up and down the Sierras in the western United States and British Columbia, on both slopes, and as far north as the headwaters of the Mackenzie River. The occurrence of hard wood in the Great Interior Basin and of yew and other soft woods on the western slopes gave rise to the wide, thin bow in the latter, and the long, ovate, sectioned bow in the basin.

The *sinew-corded bow* has a backing made of a long string or braid of sinew, passing to and fro along the back. Practically speaking, there were four classes of this corded or laced pattern. In the most primitive of these the sinew cord, or yarn, is made fast to one nock and passed backward and forward along the back of the compound bow forty or fifty times. Additional strength is given by half turns and short excursions to and fro on the back of the grip.

In a slightly more complex design, this bow is of wood, broad, flat, and straight, but narrowed and thickened at the grip. The back is flat and the belly often keeled, and frequently a stiffener of wood or antler is glued under the sinew lining. In this type the strands of sinew cord lie parallel, passing entirely from end to end, the last one wrapped spirally around the rest.

The *Arctic type bow* is shorter and narrower, the ends are often bent in, and strips of sealskin are put under

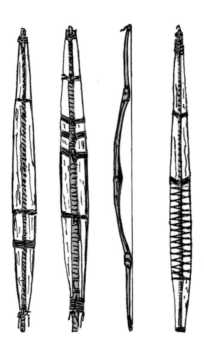

the backing. The cord—always braided sinew—passes from nock to nock.

The *Western type bow* is broader and flatter than the last, but less contracted at the grip. The backing is in three parts, none of which extend as far as the nocks. The first cable goes from end to end near the nocks; the second goes from elbow to elbow, approximately a foot from each nock; and the third goes along the straight part of the back. The cables become practically one along the grip.

Arrows

Basically, the arrow is a straight rod pointed at one end and hardened—perhaps in the fire—feathered and notched at the other end for the bowstring. But the arrow is best understood by breaking it down into its constituent parts.

Parts of the Arrow

The *shaft* is the main body of the arrow.

Shaftment is that part of the shaft on which the feather is fastened. This section of the arrow varies in length, in form, and in ornamentation, because it is the part of the weapon upon which designs and other ornamental marks were usually placed.

Feathering are the strips of feather or other thin material lain on at the butt of the arrow to stabilize its flight. The feathers of an arrow are usually taken from the wing or tail feathers of predator birds, though others were sometimes used. The feather is carefully split from one end to the other, and the pith and unnecessary parts of the quill carefully removed, so as to leave the plume and only a strip of the midrib. In laying the feather on the arrow shaft, differences of manipulation existed among the different tribes. In some of them the midrib was laid close to the shaftment and glued tight, while the ends were seized with sinew, and the plume was shorn very close to the shaftment in a parallel line.

The *nock* is the back end of the arrow that is seized by the fingers in releasing. This is an important feature of this weapon. For instance, the Inuit peoples' arrows have flat nocks, while most other arrows in the world seem to be more or less cylindrical or spherical. In some the form is T-shaped; in others, rounded like a bulb; in others, cylindrical; and in others, spreading, like the tail of a fish or swallow.

The *notch* is the cut made at the back end of the shaftment of the arrow to receive the bowstring.

The *foreshaft* is that piece of hard wood, bone, or antler laid into the front portion of the shaft and trimmed to a shape conforming to the width of the shaft. It served the double purpose of making the front of the arrow heavier than the rear, and it also afforded a better means of attaching arrowheads or harpoon barbs.

The *head* is the front part of an arrow that makes the wound. Arrowheads differ from one another in material, in size, in form, and in methods of attachment. The Native American arrow-maker was something of a mineralogist. He not only knew the qualities of rocks and the best methods of working them, but he also knew the best conditions in which they existed for his purposes in his environment. The arrowhead might also be of bone or horn.

Shooting an Arrow

An arrow is always drawn the full length of the shaft, no matter how distant the target, thus the length of the any given arrow conforms to the size and strength of the bow.

Arrow Releases

Native peoples employed four releases, again, depending on the type of the arrow and the size and strength of the bow.

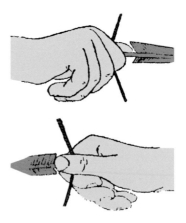

Held by the thumb and first joint of the forefinger pinching the arrow nock, as above.

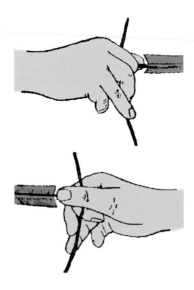

Held by the thumb and second joint of forefinger, middle finger also on string as above.

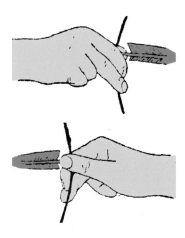

Held by the thumb, and three fingers on the string as above.

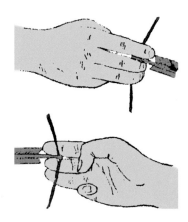

Held by the fore and middle fingers on the string as above.

Arrow Shafts

The arrow shafts are not less important than the heads. They should be straight, strong, and heavy, and for this reason year-old shoots of the dogwood, cherry, or serviceberry make the best arrow-wood. The Native peoples of the Southwest use reeds of cane, and with them the shaft is often composed of three or more pieces. Some tribes use shoots of the willow, but this warps so readily and is so light and weak that it will hardly be employed if any other wood can be had.

The length and thickness of the shaft varies with the tribe—as does the manner of feathering, of fastening on the arrowhead, and of painting—but it almost always has two or three winding grooves throughout its length, the purpose of which is said to be to facilitate the flow of blood, and probably also the arrow's entrance into the flesh.

The arrow shafts, after being cut and scraped free from bark, are bound tightly together in bundles and hung up to dry in the lodge, where it is warm. When partly seasoned, they are taken down and worked over. Those that are not entirely straight are manipulated— bent back and forth. If a likely shaft is still not straight, it may be greased and heated over a fire and worked again until it is perfectly straight. Then the bundle is again hung up and left until the wood is thoroughly seasoned. A little while later the shafts are again examined and the bad ones are rejected.

Usually they are reduced to the proper thickness by scraping with a bit of flint or with a knife, but often a slab of grooved sandstone is used for this purpose. This has the same effect as if they were sandpapered down. In order to make the grooves in the shaft, it is passed through a hole bored through bone or antler, or sometimes, it is said, by pressure of the teeth, in which the wood is held while being bent. This hole is just large enough for the shaft to pass through and is circular, except for one or two projections, which press into the wood and cut out the grooves. The feathers are usually three in number, attached with tree resin or glue, but also tied above and below with sinew. The notch for the string is deep and on the same plane as the arrow's head. The feathers are rarely two or four, and their length varies. They are usually taken from birds of prey.

Arrow-Making Materials
(A)   A likely stick for the shaft
(B)   Flint for the arrowhead
(C)   Sinew for binding the arrowhead and for feathering
(D)   Resin or glue
(E)   Ground color for paint mixture
(F)   Feathers

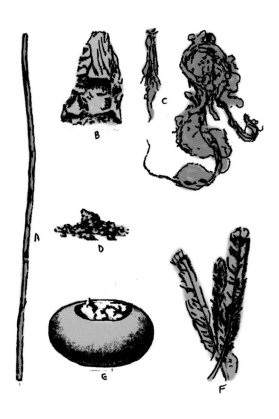

Making Arrowheads

As with stone blades, covered in Chapter One: Tool Kits, the materials used most often for arrowhead construction were flint, chert, and obsidian—either obtained locally or by trading with other tribes.

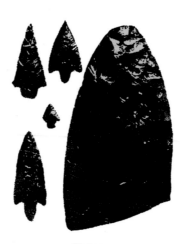

The blanks for the arrowhead are initially struck from a large block, or core-stone, by light sharp blows of a small hammerstone, as in *percussion flaking*, or by the application of force by an antler tool, as in *pressure flaking*.

Sometimes these blocks were first "sweated" by being buried in wet earth, over which a fire was built. The object of this treatment was to bring to light any cracks and checks in the stone, so that no unnecessary labor was performed on a piece too badly cracked to be profitably worked.

As the blanks are struck off, the blocks of stone are turned, so that after a while they become roughly cylindrical, growing smaller and smaller, until at length each block is too small to furnish more blanks. They are then put aside.

The blanks are now examined. Some are rejected at once, others are judged satisfactory.

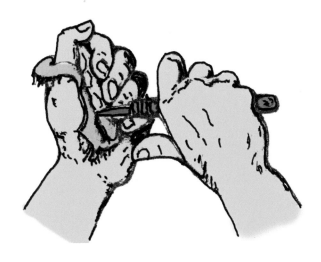

Pressure Flaking an Arrowhead

The arrow-maker covers the palm of the hand that is to hold the blank—usually his left hand—with a piece of hide resembling a "sail-maker's palm," and with his tool of antler in the other hand, he begins to press it against the side of the blank, flaking off one chip, then another close to it. He passes along the edge of the unformed flint repeating this procedure until one side of it is sharp and more or less straight, and then along the other, taking special care when working the point. Carelessness or haste here endangers the arrowhead; for if its point should be broken, it is good for nothing.

Given their small size, arrowheads are rarely fluted as spear-blades are, but they are often *tanged* for ease in seating them into the shaft. They are often *notched* as well.

Both these processes are usually performed using an anvil stone of one size or another to work the blank on, rather than in the hand. Tanging is most often done through a process of pressure flaking, while notching is usually accomplished by pecking.

Once the head is shaped, there are often left some thin projecting edges, marring its symmetry and adding nothing to its effectiveness. These are broken off either by pressure flaking or by pecking.

There was a wide variation in the shape and size of these stone points. Some were very small, others large, some fine and delicate, and others coarse and clumsy. The edges were usually regular and fairly smooth, but sometimes serrated. A wound inflicted by one of

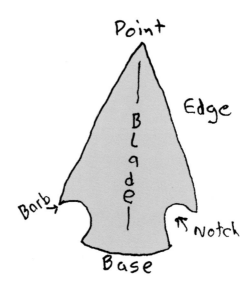

them is said to have been much more serious than one inflicted by a straight-edged point. The serrated stone point makes a ragged wound, and the point, if deeply buried in the flesh, could not easily be extracted nor pushed through, and would readily become detached from the arrow shaft.

These arrowheads were roughly triangular in shape but often had a short shank for attachment to the shaft. This shank, or the middle part of the base of the triangle, was set into a notch in the shaft, fastened by glue made from the hoofs of the buffalo, and made secure by lashing it in place by fine sinew strings, put on wet.

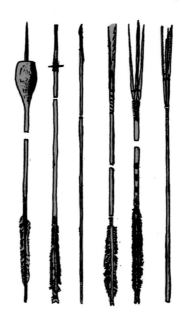

Retrieving Arrows

A retrieving arrow was one with a—usually bone— barbed head, designed for recovering fish or burrowing game. They often differed from stone-pointed hunting and war arrows in that they tended to have longer shafts, were often attached to fishing line or other cord, and were shot from less robust bows.

Bowstrings

The bowstring among the North American tribes was made of the following:

- Strips of tough rawhide, plain or twisted.
- String made of the best fibers of the country—hemp, etc.
- The intestines of animals cut into strips and twisted.

But most frequently, they were made from the strip of sinew extending from the head along the back (backstrap), and also those taken from the lower part of the legs of deer and other ruminants were selected. These were hung up to dry. For making bowstrings the gristle was shredded with the fingers in fibers as fine as silk in some tribes but coarser in others. These fibers were twisted into yarn on the thigh by means of the palm of the hand. (See the section on cording in Chapter One: Tool Kits.)

CHAPTER THREE: SHELTER

Shelter is a key concern when it comes to the survival of an individual or of a people. Design and construction depended on the available resources and upon the other imperatives of usage and cultural tradition.

TIPI

One of the most characteristic shelters of plains peoples was the tipi, and all the tribes of the area, almost without exception, used it for at least a part of the year. Primarily, the tipi was a conical tent covered with dressed buffalo skins.

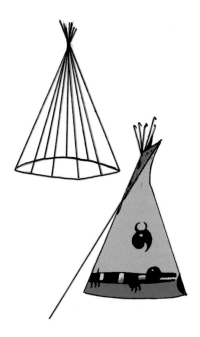

First, a conical framework of long slender poles was erected and the cover was then raised into place. Then the edges of the cover were staked down and the poles supporting the "ears" were put in place. The "ears" are wings, or flies, to keep the wind out of the smoke hole at the top; they were adjusted by the outside poles. The fire was built near the center and the beds were spread upon the ground around the sides. The head of the family usually bedded near the rear, opposite, or facing the door.

Bark-Covered Tipis

It is important to note that the use of the tipi was not confined to the plains. The Ojibway along the Great Lakes used it, but they covered it with birch bark, as did also many of the Cree and tribes of eastern Canada and New England. Even the Santee-Dakota used birch bark for tipi covers. To the north, among the Lake Winnipeg Chippeways, the tipi covering is also of birch bark, which, when readied for transportation, is in seven rolls. The largest and longest when unrolled reaches around the lodge poles at the ground from one side of the door to the other; the one next in length fits around the lodge poles above the lower strip, lapping

a little over it, so as to shed the rain. One still shorter goes on above this, and so onto the top of the cone. At both ends of each strip there is a lath-like stick of wood to keep the bark from fraying or splitting. The pieces of which these strips are composed are neatly sewed together with tamarack root. There are no wings or ears around the smoke holes of this kind of lodge, but these are not needed.

A tipi-like skin-covered tent was in general use among the Indians of Labrador and westward throughout Canada. In the West, the plains tipi was found among the Nez Perce, Flathead, Cayuse, and Umatilla; to the southwest, it was found among the Apache. It is nearly impossible to determine what tribes first originated this type of shelter, though a comparison of the details of structure might give some definite clues. Yet, it is clear that it was especially adapted to the roving life of the plains tribes when pursuing the buffalo.

EARTHEN LODGES

Before going further, we must remember that the tipi was not the only type of shelter used by these Indians. The Mandan, Hidatsa, and Arikara lived in more or less permanent villages of sod- and earth-covered lodges. The following description of a Hidatsa house may serve as a type.

> "On the site of a proposed lodge, they often dig
> down a foot or more in order to find earth compact
> enough to form a good floor; but in some lodges,
> the floors are lower than the general surface of the
> ground on which the village stands. The floor is of
> earth, and has in its center a circular depression, for

a fire-pit, about a foot deep, and three or four feet wide, with an edging of flat rocks. These dwellings, were from thirty to forty feet in diameter, from ten to fifteen feet high in the center, and from five to seven feet high at the eaves, and were quite commodious."

Framing an Earthen Lodge

A number of stout posts, from ten to fifteen, according to the size of the lodge, and rising to the height of about five feet above the surface of the earth, were set about ten feet apart in a circle. On the tops of these posts, solid beams are laid, extending from one to another. Then, toward the center of the lodge, four more posts are erected, of much greater diameter than the outer posts, and rising to the height of ten or more feet above the ground. These four posts stand in the corners of a square of about fifteen feet, and their tops are connected with four heavy beams laid horizontally. From the four central beams to the smaller external beams, long poles

served as rafters and were stretched at an angle of about thirty degrees to the horizon; and from the outer beams to the earth a number of shorter poles were laid in at an angle of about forty-five degrees. Finally, a number of saplings or rails were laid horizontally to cover the space between the four central beams, leaving only a hole for the combined skylight and chimney. This frame was then covered with willows, hay, and earth.

Dwellings of approximately the same type were used by the Pawnee, Omaha, Ponca, Kansas, Missouri, and Oto.

DOME-SHAPED LODGES

The Osage, on the other hand, are credited with the use of dome-shaped wigwams covered with mats and bark—like the Ojibway and other woodland peoples. The Hidatsa type of lodge is, unlike the tipi, definitely localized along the Missouri and the Platte and suggests that it must have originated within this territory. The Omaha claim to have originally used tipis and to have learned the use of earthen lodges from the Ankara. However, many tribes used tipis when on summer and winter buffalo hunts.

SOD HOUSES

The Pawnees, Arickaras, and Mandans built large sod houses. The Wichitas built beehive-like dwellings of grass; the hogans of the Navajoes were of brush and sticks; both walls and roofs of the houses of the North-west Coast Indians are made of shakes, split from the cedar. On the whole, the difference between the homes of the various tribes is very great.

WOODEN HOUSES

Some of the Santee-Dakota peoples lived for a part of the year in rectangular cabins of bark and poles, as did many of the eastern woodland tribes in their Long Houses. In the West, an oval or conical brush and grass shelter seems to have preceded the tipi. The Comanche used both this western type of brush lodge as well as the tipi. The northern Shoshone mixed brush and bark lodges as well as tipis in the same camp.

The western tribes, raising maize and other crops, used earth or bark houses, but as a rule lived in them only while planting, tending, and harvesting the crop. For the most part the Natives of the West lived in skin lodges. This was partly because these dwellings were warm and dry, and their material for construction was easily obtained, but it was especially because they were light and convenient and could readily be moved about from place to place, and so were in that respect well suited to the needs of a nomadic people. But not all the Indians were dwellers in tents. By Contact the evolution of the house had progressed far beyond the single-roomed shelter of grass or bark or skins.

Many Native peoples of the East had large connected houses of poles, which were sometimes fortified. The Pawnees and Mandans built great sod or dirt houses, in which many families lived in common; the sleeping places around the walls were separated by permanent wooden partitions, with a curtain of hide or cloth suspended in front of each so as to form an actual room.

MOBILE HOMES

Various traditions suggest that many tribes, who at the time of Contact lived in portable lodges—either of bark or hide—once had permanent houses, and that the near-exclusive use of skin lodges among the plains peoples may have come about in comparatively recent times. The coming of the horse and the expansion of cultures based upon the buffalo put a premium on mobility, and many of these tribes may have lived on the plains for a short time only—say two or three centuries—having migrated from some earlier homeland. It seems probable that some of those peoples we have come to regard as nomadic may have lost different arts of building, which they had once practiced. Indeed, many of them have traditions of a time when they lived in permanent dwellings, though usually the stories are so vague that little can be gleaned of the character of these dwellings. The Pawnees say that in their ancient home—which was probably on the Pacific slope—they dwelt in houses built of stone.

PUEBLOS

Farther to the south, the peoples of the Pueblo culture lived in many-roomed, many-storied houses made of stone, one dwelling abutting on another, which may be the most complex style of dwelling among the Native Americans north of Mexico. This design made sense in a climate that tended to be hot in the daytime and cold at night. These communities were also highly dependent on agriculture, so a more or less fixed residence made good sense.

ARCTIC AND SUBARCTIC DWELLINGS

The Inuit and other peoples of the far north built their more or less permanent dwellings by digging a large pit well into the ground—during the short summer—and constructing a dome lattice of wood and bark over it. Soon the snows came and covered all, making for a snug, cozy dwelling. Entry and exit was through a hole in the top and, from within, accessed by ladder.

When following the caribou herds, the hunters lived in domed tents of bent, dried poles, all covered with tanned caribou skins. The whole thing was easily taken down and loaded on a dogsled when the herd moved on.

Igloo

Despite the popular idea, this shelter was not universally used by the peoples of the far north. Only certain Arctic groups built igloos, and then only during the seal-hunting season.

Building a Simple Igloo

Mark out the circular shape of the igloo in the packed snow.

Standing outside the circle, excavate the snow within by cutting it into blocks. These will be used to form the walls.

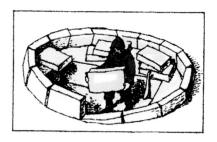

Place the blocks in ever shorter, spiraling rows, against and on top of each other, raising the walls in a dome.

Finish the igloo by excavating an entrance, taking care to leave a small hole in the top for an air vent.

NORTHWEST COAST LODGES

The Native Americans of the Northwest Coast built their lodges employing a post and beam construction with a sheathing of shakes and boards split from the plentiful wood of the region. These houses might be very simple, shed-like affairs, or they might be considerably more lavish, with dug-out interiors and ornate plank flooring. The general design within the dwelling

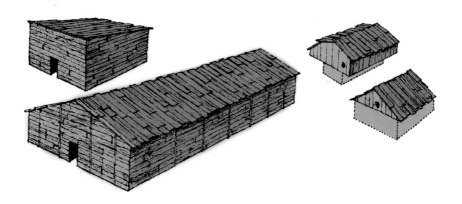

was reminiscent in style of traditional Japanese architecture, and bespeaks obvious cultural contact.

GULF COAST DWELLINGS

Native Americans like the Florida Seminoles and other Gulf Coast peoples tended to live a hunter-gatherer lifestyle. Their houses were correspondingly simple: a roof of reeds to keep out the rain and a raised platform to secure them from the flood.

CHAPTER FOUR: TRANSPORT

For the thousands of years before Contact—before the horse was introduced—the Native peoples of North America traveled either on foot or by water. In a world without roads or wheels, the lakes, rivers, and streams served as natural highways.

CANOES

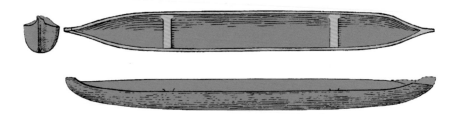

Dugout Canoes

The most complex canoe used by the Native peoples of America is the birch bark, yet in many respects the dugout canoe equals or excels it. It is of one piece of wood and is much more substantial than the bark canoe, which, taken all in all, is a frail vessel.

Making a Dugout Canoe

After the tree trunk has been chosen and felled, the trunk is stripped of its bark and is flattened along the top and roughly shaped.

Then the work of hollowing it out begins. Fires are built on the top side of the log, carefully watched, and controlled so that they burn evenly and slowly down into the wood. When they have gone far enough, they

are extinguished, and the burned matter is scraped away. This is repeated as needed. Then the canoe-builder, using a wooden mallet and a stone chisel, carefully goes over the whole surface. At each blow he takes off a little chip of wood, as large as a man's thumb and quite thin; this he continues, within and without, until the canoe is shaped. It is then braced by two or more crosspieces, which span the gunwales on either side and are sewn into place. This prevents the sides from spreading. Only seasoned and perfect timber is used for these canoes.

Bark Canoes

Though not as durable as the dugout canoe, nor as easily constructed, the great advantage of a bark canoe is its lightness. It is the vessel of choice when traveling up and down waterways. Where portaging is necessary, it was the perfect vessel. The canoe may be of any length.

One of fifteen or twenty feet can easily be carried on the shoulders of two men; while a smaller one, ten or twelve feet long, can be managed by one man without much difficulty.

In regions where birch was not readily available, canoes were often fashioned of spruce bark.

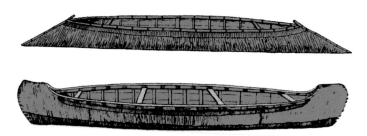

Building a Birch-Bark Canoe

The bark can be harvested in one of two ways: either by felling a tree—this permits you to strip it easily and makes real sense if you intend to use the wood of the tree in your construction—or by stripping it from a standing tree.

The birch tree is selected for straightness, smoothness, freedom from knots or limbs, toughness of bark, and size—though this is not so important, as you will likely need to piece out the sides.

Bark can be peeled when the sap is flowing or when the tree is not frozen, at any time in late spring, summer, and early fall—it is called summer bark—or in winter during a thaw, again, when the tree is not frozen, and when the sap has begun to flow.

Summer bark peels readily, is smooth inside, and is of a yellow color, which turns reddish when exposed to the sun. Winter bark adheres closely to the tree and often brings up part of the inner bark, which on exposure turns dark red. This rough surface ought to be moistened and scraped away.

After the bark has been peeled, the inside surface can be warmed with a torch, which softens and makes it supple. This torch was often made of a bundle of birch bark, wound around a stick.

The harvested bark is then rolled up like a carpet, with inside surface out, tightly bound, and carried to the worksite. Lay it in the shade where the sunshine will not harden it. The first effect of heat is to make it pliant, but long exposure to heat or to dry atmosphere makes it hard and brittle.

The gunwales of the canoe are composed of four lengths of cedar or some similar wood, about a quarter-inch thick by an inch or more in width—two for each side—one to go on the inside edge and one for the outside. The width and shape of the vessel is determined by the length of the cross pieces used in separating the sides of the gunwale frame.

Lay the bark on flat ground with the weathered side up. Weigh the center down with several good-sized rounded stones. The part that forms the bottom of the canoe should be one whole piece. If it is not large enough, pieces of the bark are sewn onto it.

Measure out the length of the canoe, and at each end, close together, drive two stakes firmly into the ground. The bark is then folded on the middle line, with inside of the bark outward, and inserted between the two stakes. The ends of the bark should extend beyond the stakes far enough to facilitate the fashioning of curved bows at each end of the canoe.

On each side drive several stakes into the ground, closely corresponding to the shape of the gunwale frame and lay it atop the stakes. This will allow the edges of the bark to be brought up, folded over, and fastened with a winding stitch to the frame.

Now lash the ends of the gunwale frames together, and adjust and lash the cross pieces to the gunwale. This will largely determine the overall shape of the canoe.

Mark out the contour of the bows and cut the bark into that shape, then stitch the pieces together, cover the edge with a folded strip of bark, and stitch again. Stiffen the bow by bending and wedging a three-foot long, one inch by one quarter inch, cedar lath inside the bow(s). Lash to the underside of the gunwale ends and seat it with resin or pitch.

Remove the stone weights and stiffen the bark by lining the inside with long thin strips of cedar. They should be placed longitudinally, lap where their ends meet, and be seated with pine pitch or resin.

The knees or ribs are made of strips of ash or any wood that is firm and elastic, and should be about one quarter-inch thick by two or more inches. They ride perpendicularly to the cedar lining, are bent down to the bottom, and are lashed to the gunwale frame. They should be placed close together along the whole length of the canoe. Smear the inside and all the seams with pine pitch or resin.

Sea-Going Canoes of the Northwest Coast

Since the Native peoples of the Northwest Coast got the greater part of their living from the sea—from fishing and whaling—they needed a much more robust vessel than the bark canoes of the inland peoples. Instead they built large dugout canoe-like boats, hewn from the giant redwoods and other trees of their region. In size they might be anywhere from fifteen feet to thirty feet long, or longer even—ships, in all but name. The rough ocean waters meant they needed a craft with a really high bow and stern. They used a technique whereby the bow and stern sections were carved separately and afterwards pieced or fitted onto the body of the boat.

Constructing a Sea-Going, Dugout Canoe

After the tree is fallen, it is split lengthwise, making two prospective hulls.

The bark is shaved away and the sides are shaped.

The bottom or keel is carved flat all along its length, giving the boat a shallow draft.

The hull is then turned over and work begins on carving out the inside. The techniques used here are much like those employed by the inland peoples in the making of their dugouts. Fire is used to break down the inner wood, and the inside is chopped and carved away.

The boatwright takes care to see that the sides, though not too thick, remain robust. After the hull has been hollowed out, it is filled with boiling water to soften the sides, and thwarts are wedged and tapped into place, slowly widening the interior.

The high bow and stern pieces, which have been separately carved, are then fitted tightly into place, glued with tree resin, and pegged with dowels.

The whole is sanded with rough-grained stone and the vessel is painted, sometimes very elaborately.

Seal-Skin Canoes of the Far North

Kayaks

The Native peoples of the far north fashioned their hunting boats of driftwood and sealskin. The best known of these vessels was the Aleut kayak, or *baidarka*, a relatively short, one-man boat, either two-beaked or with one beak and a square stern—usually with a single cockpit amidships. The top was covered in sealskin as well and rimmed with a wooden collar, creating a water-tight seal. It was propelled with a double paddle.

When fully equipped for seal hunting, this kayak carried on its deck a harpoon, an atlatl (throwing board), a stabbing spear, and an inflated sealskin buoy of seal-bladder, which was attached to the kill to give it added buoyancy for the long tow back to camp.

Umiaks

Another type of watercraft favored by the Native peoples of the far north was the Eskimo Umiak, sometimes called "woman's boat." This vessel was also of seal or walrus skin, stretched on a driftwood frame, and might be anywhere from twelve to forty feet long.

Not a hunting boat, its purpose was to transport possessions and supplies. It was ordinarily propelled using single-bladed paddles, or it was towed by kayak. Both the kayak and the umiak were coastal vessels and did not venture far out to sea.

Bull Boats

The Native peoples of the plains, and of the West generally, made little use of canoes. It seems probable that the ease of travel on the open plains and the fact that the buffalo were to be found inland made the use of canoes impractical, whereas along the Great Lakes, in the lake districts of the Midwest, and in the Eastern regions, the broad expanses of water offered every advantage to their use. The tribes living along the Mississippi made some use of canoes, according to early accounts, while those of the Missouri and inland used only simple tub-like vessels for the purposes of ferrying themselves across rivers and streams. These were called bull boats and were made by stretching buffalo hides over a wooden frame.

Building a Bull Boat

Willows grow upon the banks of many streams and can be bent into the desired shape. To make a boat with one hide, a number of straight willows are cut about an inch in diameter. Then the ends are sharpened and driven into the ground, forming a framework in the shape of a half an eggshell, and cut through the longitudinal axis. Where these rods cross they are firmly tied.

A stout rod is then heated and bent around the frame in such a way that the edges of the hide, when laid over it and drawn tight, will just reach it.

This rod forms the gunwale, which is then tied to the ribs.

Small rods are then fitted in so as to make it symmetrical and strong. Then the green or soaked hide is pulled over the edges, sewed to the gunwales, and left to dry.

The rods are then cut off, even with the gunwale, and the boat is ready for use.

SNOWSHOES

The first thing is to plan the size, shape, and general character of the shoes, making the frames, or bows, are the first steps.

The tree from which the frames are to be made should be not more than eight inches in diameter,

and one of six inches is better. It should have droop-
ing branches and ought to have eight or ten feet of the
trunk straight and clean, free of limbs, and absolutely
without a twist to the grain.

After the tree has been felled and a section of the
proper length cut off, a groove about one and a half
inches deep is carefully cut along the entire length of
one side. Take care not to strike hard, as that might
injure the wood.

When the groove is finished a similar one is cut on
the opposite side. The stick should be split with wooden
wedges, and if it is properly done, the split will follow the grooves. The best half should then be chosen
for the proposed snowshoe frames, and this should be
ripped lengthwise with a saw, or split, as desired. Each
of the pieces will make a frame or bow.

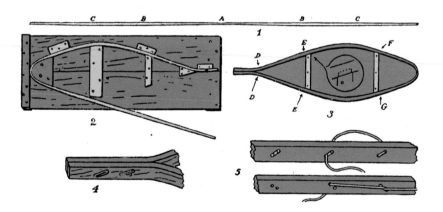

One side of the stick is then cut and planed until it is
perfectly straight—its face at a right angle to the bark
side. There should be nothing taken off the bark side,
not even the bark, until after the wood is bent into
shape for the snowshoe frame.

Next, the third side of the stick is marked off with
a marking gauge and either cut or sawed to the mark.

The fourth side, the inside of the stick, which will be the inside of the finished frame, is then cut down to the proper dimensions; but on this side an even thickness is not maintained, the toe portion being cut thinnest, with the heel—ends of the stick—coming next.

For a snowshoe of average size, say forty-four inches in length and fourteen inches wide, the stick should measure eight and a half feet in length, one inch in width, seven-eighths-inch thick at the parts that will become the middle of the shoe (B to C in figure one), one-half inch at A, and about five-eighths inch at the ends.

Before anything more can be done with the wood, a form for bending the frames must be made. A convenient form is shown in figure two. For steaming the wood properly, it is necessary to have a steaming box, which is merely a long case made of narrow boards, open at both ends. The stick is placed in this case, and the steam from a boiling tea kettle is turned in one end so that the hot steam travels the entire length. The wood should be steamed for an hour, and then it is ready for bending.

Figure two shows how the wood is bent and secured on the form. The toe must be formed very carefully, bending only a little at first, then releasing, then bending a little more, and so on until the wood can be easily and safely bent to complete shape and secured by nailing blocks to the form. The wood should be allowed to dry thoroughly on the form before filling, which will require at least two weeks.

After the frames are dry they may be taken from the form, with the tail end of each fastened and the crossbars fitted into place. The ends may be secured with a wood screw until after the frames have been strung, but the screw should then be removed and the ends tied with rawhide, through gimlet holes, the part between being counter sunk so that the thongs will be protected from wear. This is shown in figure four.

The crossbars are pieces of flat, strong wood, about one and a fourth-inch wide and nearly a half-inch thick, with rounded edges. These should be placed about sixteen or seventeen inches apart, measuring from center to center, and so placed that when the frame is suspended on the hands midway between these two sticks, the tail will outweigh the toe by just a few ounces. These crossbars should be carefully mortised into the frame as shown in the small diagram in the center of figure three.

In both sides of the frame from D to E, also from F to G, gimlet holes are bored through the bows from outside to inside at intervals of two inches, or a little more, the holes being in pairs obliquely placed and countersunk between. Three holes are also bored through each crossbar, as shown.

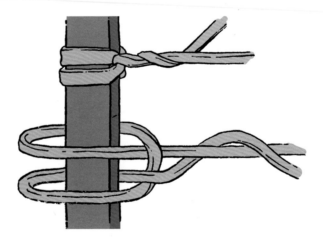

The frames are now ready for filling. Regarding material for filling, for ordinary use, there is nothing equal to cowhide, which is a fairly heavy skin. A whole hide will fill several pairs of shoes. The portion along the back is best, and this should be used for filling the middle section. The lighter parts from the edges of the skin will do for stringing the heels and toes. All strands should be cut length-wise of the skin and full length— their width depending on the thickness of the skin. It is well to cut several trial widths, so that the proper weight of strand may be determined. For a coarse webbed shoe, the thongs, after being stretched and dried, should be about five-sixteenths of an inch wide for the middle portion of the shoe; for the ends, an eighth inch is sufficiently heavy. These strands of hide should all be soaked and stretched thoroughly, allowed to dry while stretched, soaked again just before using, and then strung into the frames while wet.

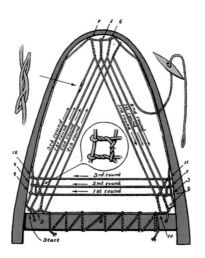

The ends are filled first. A strand of the water-soaked rawhide is stretched tightly around the inside of the toe portion through the little gimlet holes, as shown in figure five, starting and finishing at one of the holes in the forward crossbar. This thong is called the lanyard, and its purpose is to hold the filling, which is woven into the toe.

A small needle of very hard wood, or bone, is used for filling the ends. Starting in the lower left-hand corner, it goes up to the part marked 1, passes around the lanyard, twists back around itself about an inch, and then goes down to 2, there passing around the lanyard and again twisting around itself, then around the lanyard at 3, a single twist, and then across to 4, where it again turns around the lanyard, then twists down around the first strand to the starting point, under the lanyard at 5 and up to 6. From there the strand loops and twists the same as in the first round, except that at the lower corners it loops back around the first round, then twists around itself, then around the lanyard, and on the same as before. This looping back of every second round is continued until the filling extends across the entire forward part of the toe, when it is discontinued, and each round is made like the first. This looping back throws the filling alternately from side to side.

The filling must be stretched in very tightly and must not be allowed to slip. When one strand is used up another is joined on in the manner shown. See that every round crosses the others in the proper way, and all the twists are made alike. The weave will finish at the center of the crossbar.

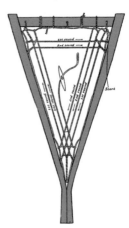

The filling in the tail end or heel starts at the upper right-hand corner and finishes in the middle of the crossbar. Great care should be used to get the twists and loops right, and to see that the thongs cross in the proper way.

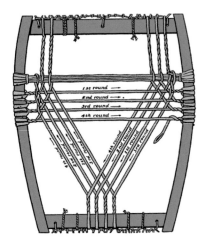

Filling the middle section is simpler than it appears at first glance—it is practically a repetition of the system used in the toe portion. The edges of the wood should be rounded slightly to prevent them cutting the thongs.

While the system of stringing this part may appear quite intricate, it is in reality simple; it is the more elaborate arrangement of the forward portion that makes this section appear so complicated. The stout bunch of thongs shown in the drawing, known as the toe cord, is strung in first. The rawhide strand is tightly stretched and crosses the frame some four or five times, with a loop being thrown around the whole on the inside of the frame on both sides in the last round. This should be so executed that the last loop will be on the right-hand side. The thong then loops around this bunch of cords again about an inch from the frame, and from there is strung up around the crossbar, then twists around itself back to the starting point. From there it passes down diagonally to the center of the rear crossbar, where it loops and twists again, then moves up to the upper left-hand corner, where it twists up the same as on the opposite side. From here it will be noted the thong runs down a short distance and loops around the left side of the frame. The simple loop used for this purpose is clearly shown in a small drawing. From this loop the rawhide strand twists back about an inch, then runs straight across the shoe to the right, where the loop is repeated. This completes the first round of the filling.

The second round starts in about the same way as the first, goes up to the crossbar at the left of the first round, twists back to the toe cord, moves from there to the rear crossbar, then goes up to the left-hand corner. Here the system changes, for the strand is run up and twisted around the toe cord and the first round of filling before it is looped to the frame. After looping, it is brought across to the right, where it again loops and twists, and then twists around the toe cord and the first round of filling exactly as on the left, after which it is run down to the rear crossbar. In this way the stringing continues, every second round twisting forward around the preceding two. This binds the filling firmly and, it will be noted, also alternates the successive rounds from side to side. When the process of filling has progressed so far that there are four twists around the forward crossbar, on each side, this twisting should be stopped and the remainder of the forward portion left open, for this is where the foot of the wearer works through when walking. This open space should measure about four and a half inches in width, and if it does not, the filling must be shifted. In very coarse, meshed shoes, three twists on each side will be all that can be given. An extra turn around the toe cord should also be made on each of these two twists of the filling, for considerable strain is thrown onto this portion.

From this point on, instead of running forward and twisting around the crossbar, the filling simply twists around the toe cord. Be careful to keep the filling smooth and the toe cord flat, otherwise sore feet will result from wearing the shoes. The weave finishes in the center of the toe cord, and there the end of the thong should be securely and neatly fastened. The last touch is to wind a strand of rawhide about the twisted thongs on each side of the foot opening and around the toe cord, which makes these parts smooth and protects them from wear.

In the drawings of the heel and toe sections, it will be noted that I have shown the web tied to the crossbars with twine. This is not a permanent feature, for when the center of the shoe has been filled these strings may be removed.

Snowshoes require care, not only while in use, but at other times as well, because they are strung

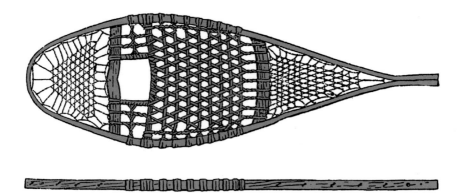

with rawhide, a material very susceptible to heat and moisture. If the shoes are not dried thoroughly after becoming wet, the stringing will rot, while if dried too rapidly, the filling becomes brittle and breaks when put to a strain. Native Americans were careful to keep their snowshoes in good repair and snug and dry in the lodge when not in use.

BUILDING AN INDIAN TOBOGGAN

The first need is a board about eight feet in length and sixteen or more inches in width. Oak is the best wood for this purpose, although hickory, basswood, or ash will do excellently. It should be planed or sawed to a thickness of about a third of an inch, and should be free of knots. If a single board of the required width is not easily found, two boards may be used and secured side by side by three cleats, one at each end and the other in the middle. A single board is much preferred, if it can be had.

Next, seven or eight wooden crosspieces of a length equivalent to the width of the board are needed. Four old broomsticks, cut in the required lengths, will do the trick perfectly, and if these are not available, other sticks of similar dimensions should be used.

The two side pieces are needed next. These should be about five feet in length and of a thickness exactly similar to the crosspieces.

Next procure a few pairs of leather shoestrings or some strips of tough calfskin. With these collected we now begin the work of putting the parts together.

Begin by laying the crosspieces at equal distances along the board; across these and near their ends, lay the two side pieces, as seen in the illustration.

Using a drill, bore four holes through the board, beneath the end of each crosspiece, and also directly under the side piece. It's a good idea to mark the various points for the holes with a pencil, after which the sticks can be removed and the work much more easily performed. The four holes should be about an inch apart, or so disposed as to mark the four corners of a square inch.

It is also necessary to make other holes along the length of the crosspieces, as seen in the illustration.

The line on these can also be marked with the pencil across the board, and the holes can be made afterwards.

These should also be an inch apart, and only two in number at each point, one on each side of the stick.

When all the holes are completed, turn the board over, in order to complete preparations on the other side.

The object of these various holes is for the passage of the leather shoestrings we will use to secure the crosspieces firmly to the board.

In order to prevent these loops from wearing off on the under side, make small grooves on the underside connecting the holes. This allows the leather string to sink into the wood, where it will be protected from injury. A narrow chisel is the best tool for this purpose.

When the under side is finished, the board may be turned over and the crosspieces and sides again arranged in place as described above.

Secure the pieces to the board by the leather strings through the various holes, always knotting on the upper surface, and taking care that the knots are firmly tied. The ends of all the crosspieces will require a double cross stitch through the four holes beneath, in order to secure the side pieces as well. This is plainly shown in the small diagram (*a*). The front end of each side piece underneath should now be sharpened to a point, to allow for the bend at the front of the toboggan.

The crosspiece at the front end should be secured to the *under side of the board*, so that as it bends over it will appear on the upper edge, as in the illustration. The board should then be bent with a graceful curve, and thus held in position by a rope or strip of leather at each extremity of the end cross piece and attached to the ends of the third cross piece.

If the bending is difficult and there is danger of breaking the board, an application of boiling water will render it pliable. The drawstrings are finally attached to the ends of the second crosspiece, and the toboggan is complete.

It may now be laden with two or three hundred pounds of buffalo meat, or all the furnishings of the lodge, and will be found to draw over the surface of the snow with perfect ease. For coasting over the crust there is nothing like it.

TRAVOIS

The *Travois,* though of a French name, is of Native American origin. It is essentially an A-frame construction and consists of two long wooden staffs (often tipi poles) lashed together at the narrower ends, and braced by lashing one or two crosspieces midway to the open end.

The width of the travois was determined by the length and placement of these bracing crosspieces. This bracing also served as a rudimentary platform upon which the load could be tied.

A travois might be pulled (depending on its size) either by dog or horse—or even by a man or woman—and was particularly useful in getting loads across broken ground.

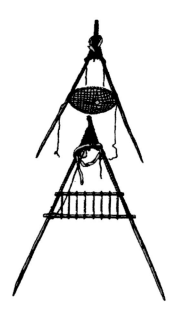

The Native peoples of the plains were more or less always on the move. All their possessions were especially designed for ready transport. Nearly all receptacles and most utensils were made of rawhide, while the tipi was easily rolled up, lashed to the travois, and hauled to the next campground.

HORSE

The horses that the Native Americans rode were invariably the wild horses, which were found in great numbers on the prairies. They had strayed from Mexico, into which they had been introduced by the Spanish invaders, and soon ranged and subsisted themselves, in winter and summer, over the vast plains of prairie that stretch from the Mexican frontiers to Lake Winnipeg in the north, a distance of three thousand miles. These horses were of small stature, of the pony order, but they were a hardy and tough animal, able to perform a continual and essential service. It is no overstatement to say that the coming of the horse to North America utterly changed the lives and cultures of the Native American peoples of the West.

The ponies were taken with the lasso, which for the Indians was a long halter or thong, made of raw-hide, of some fifteen or twenty yards in length, and which they threw with great dexterity—with a noose at one end of it—which drops over the head of the animal they wish to catch. The lasso was thrown while galloping at full speed, then the Indian dismounted from his own horse, and holding onto his end of the lasso, choked the animal down.

Scarcely a man in these regions was to be found who was not the owner of one or more of these horses—and in many instances of eight, ten, or even twenty, which he valued highly as his own personal property.

Riding Gear

The horse trappings of the plains people were rudimentary but effective.

The native bridle was a simple rope or thong looped around the jaw. Saddles were of two types: pads and frames.

The frames were made of wood or elk horn securely bound with fresh buffalo hide, which shrunk as it dried.

Women's saddles had high pommels and were often gaily ornamented.

Stirrups were also made of wood bound with rawhide.

Some peoples, the Dakota for example, used highly decorated saddle blankets, or skins; while others (Crow, Blackfoot, etc.) used elaborate cruppers.

Quirts with short handles of elk horn or wood were common.

In general, there was little difference in the form of riding gear among all the plains tribes.

CHAPTER FIVE: TRAILING

INDIAN SAGACITY—BY CAPTAIN RANDOLPH MARCY, US CAVALRY

I know of nothing in the woodman's education of so much importance, or so difficult to acquire, as the art of trailing or tracking men and animals. To become adept at this art requires the constant practice of years, and with some men a lifetime does not suffice to learn it.

Almost all the Indians whom I have met with are proficient in this species of knowledge, the faculty for acquiring which appears to be innate with them. Exigencies of woodland and prairie life stimulate him from childhood to develop faculties so important in the arts of war and of the chase.

This difficult branch of woodcraft cannot be taught from books, it is almost always a matter of practice, yet I will give some facts relating to the habits of thinking of the Indian I have known that may facilitate its acquirement.

An Indian, on coming to a trail, can generally tell at a glance its age, by what particular tribe it was made, the number of the party, and many other things connected with it astounding to the uninitiated.

I remember, upon one occasion, as I was riding with a Delaware upon the prairies, we crossed the trail of a large party of Indians traveling with lodges. The tracks appeared to me quite fresh, and I remarked to the Indian that we must be near the party. "Oh no," said he, "the trail was made two days before, in the morning," at the same time pointing with his finger to where the sun would be at about 8 o'clock. Then, seeing that my curiosity was excited to know by what means he arrived at this conclusion, he called my attention to the fact that there had been no dew for the last two nights, but that on the previous morning it had been heavy. He then pointed out to me some spears of grass that had been pressed down into the earth by the horses' hoofs, upon which the sand still adhered, having dried on, thus clearly showing that the grass was wet when the tracks were made.

At another time, as I was traveling with the same Indian, I discovered upon the ground what I took to be a bear track, with a distinctly marked impression of the heel and all the toes. I immediately called the Indian's attention to it, at the same time flattering myself that I had made quite an important discovery, which had escaped his observation. The fellow remarked with a smile, "Oh no, captain." He then pointed with his gun-rod to some spears of grass that grew near the impression, but I did not comprehend the mystery until he dismounted and explained to me that, when the wind was blowing, the spears of grass would be bent over toward the ground, and the oscillating motion thereby produced would scoop out the loose sand into the shape I have described. The truth of this explanation was apparent, yet it occurred to me that its solution would have baffled the wits of most white men.

Fresh tracks generally show moisture where the earth has been turned up, but after a short exposure to the sun they become dry. If the tracks be very recent, the sand may sometimes, where it is very loose and dry, be seen running back into the tracks, and by following them to a place where they cross water, the earth will be wet for some distance after they leave it. The droppings of the dung from animals are also good indications of the age of a trail. It is well to remember whether there have been any rains within a few days, as the age of a trail may sometimes be conjectured in this way. It is very easy to tell whether tracks have been made before or after a rain, as the water washes off all the sharp edges.

It is not a difficult matter to distinguish the tracks of American horses from those of Indian horses, as the latter are never shod; moreover, they are much smaller.

In trailing horses, there will be no trouble while the ground is soft, as the impressions they leave will then be deep and distinct; but when they pass over hard or rocky ground, it is sometimes a very slow and troublesome process to follow them. Where there is grass, the trace can be seen for a considerable time, as the grass will be trodden down and bent in the direction the party has moved; should the grass have returned to its upright position, the trail can often be distinguished by standing upon it and looking ahead for some distance in the direction it has been pursuing; the grass that has been turned over will show a different shade of green from that around it, and this often marks a trail for a long time.

Should all traces of the track be obliterated in certain localities, it is customary with the Indians to follow on in the direction it has been going for a time, and it is quite probable that in some place where the ground is more favorable it will show itself again. Should the trail not be recovered in this way, they search for a place where the earth is soft, and make a careful examination, embracing the entire area where it is likely to run.

Indians who find themselves pursued and wish to escape scatter as much as possible, with an understanding that they are to meet again at some point in advance, so that, if the pursuing party follows any one of the tracks, it will invariably lead to the place of rendezvous. If, for example, the trail points in the direction of a mountain pass, or toward any other place which affords the only passage through a particular section of country, it would not be worth while to spend much time in hunting it, as it would probably be regained at the pass.

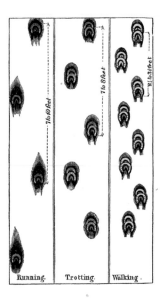

As it is important in trailing Indians to know at what gaits they are traveling, and as the appearance of the tracks of horses are not familiar to all, I have in the following cut represented the prints made by the hoofs at the ordinary speed of the walk, trot, and gallop, so that the person, in following the trail, may form an idea as to the probability of overtaking them, and regulate his movements accordingly.

In traversing a district of unknown country where there are no prominent landmarks, and with the view of returning to the point of departure, a pocket compass should always be carried, and attached by a string to a button-hole of the coat, to prevent its being lost or mislaid; and on starting out, as well as frequently during the trip, to take the bearing, and examine the appearance of the country when facing toward the starting-point, as a landscape presents a very different aspect when viewing it from opposite directions. There are few white men who can retrace their steps for any great distance unless they take the above precautions in passing over an unknown country for the first time; but with the Indians it is different; the sense of locality seems to be innate with them, and they do not require the aid of the magnetic needle to guide them.

Upon a certain occasion, when I had made a long march over an unexplored section, and was returning upon an entirely different route without neither road nor trail, a Delaware by the name of Black Beaver, who was in my party, on arriving at a particular point, suddenly halted and, turning to me, asked if I recognized the country before us. Seeing no familiar objects, I replied in the negative. He put the same question to the other white men of the party, all of whom gave the same answers, whereupon he smiled, and in his quaint vernacular said, "Injun he don't know nothing. Injun big fool. White man mighty smart; he know heap." At the same time he pointed to a tree about two hundred yards from where we were then standing, and informed us that our outward trail ran directly by the side of it, which proved to be true.

This same Black Beaver would start from any place to which he had gone by a sinuous route, through an unknown country, and keep a direct bearing back to the place of departure; and he assured me that he has never, even during the most cloudy or foggy weather, or in the darkest nights, lost his sense of direction.

I have known several men, after they had become lost in the mountains, to wander about for days without exercising the least judgment, and finally exhibiting a state of mental aberration almost upon the verge of lunacy. Instead of reasoning upon their situation, they exhaust themselves running ahead at their utmost speed without any regard to direction.

When a person is satisfied that he has lost his way, he should stop and reflect upon the course he has been traveling, the time that has elapsed since he left his camp, and the probable distance that he is from it; and if he is unable to retrace his steps, he should keep as nearly in the direction of them as possible. But, above all, he should guard against following his own track around in a circle with the idea that he is in a beaten trace.

In the night Ursa Major (the Great Bear) is not only useful to find the north star, but its position, when the pointers will be vertical in the heavens, may be estimated with sufficient accuracy to determine the north even when the north star can not be seen.

CHAPTER SIX: HUNTING

Native American hunters could read the signs of forest and stream with a degree of accuracy that to the rest of us is surprising, and they could make a fair estimate of the number and kinds of animals found in a locality.

It was essential for the successful hunter and trapper to be able to read the signs accurately. The experienced hunter knew instantly, on seeing a track, just what animal it was that passed that way and—by knowing its habits—knew about when it was likely to return. He could also tell with fair accuracy at what time the animal had passed that way, and frequently, knew whether it was a male or female, whether it was looking for food or a place of rest, whether it was on its regular route of travel, and where it was going.

BUFFALO

The Buffalo—which is actually the American Bison—was hunted both for food and for clothing in all seasons.

In the summer when their hair is short, they were hunted for food and clothing, and in the winter when it is long and heavy, they were hunted for robes, horn, bone, etc.

There were three ways of hunting this animal: by surrounding, by approaching, and by driving the herd into enclosures or traps.

Buffalo are a migratory, herding animal. They travel together across particular ranges through the different seasons. In the spring they tend to move north and northwest; in the fall east and south; in the winter east; and return to the west and north as spring approaches. They travel in herds, often in thousands.

Ancient Buffalo Hunt

The enormous numbers of buffalo that fed on the plains and in the mountains of the West made it usually an easy matter for the tribes to supply themselves with food, and yet the buffalo were not sure to be always at hand. The animals were as nomadic as the people, and sometimes moved away from a given region and did not reappear for months, so that the food stored up became entirely exhausted. They were then obliged to turn their attention to the smaller game, antelope, deer, and elk, which they could kill about their camps. However, these animals could never be relied upon. For this reason, it was the practice among many of the buffalo-eating tribes to send runners out to make long journeys to find the buffalo, and, by watching them, to learn in what direction they were tending, and then to report as quickly as possible to the camp.

When it is remembered how abundant and how unsuspicious of danger the buffalo were in the early days in the West, it might be imagined that the vigorous and active hunter—a footman who was always on the march, and nearly as swift and enduring as the buffalo—would, under ordinary conditions, have been able always to keep himself supplied with food, even though he carried only a bow and arrows as his weapon. But this was not so.

It is difficult for us who dwell among the civilized surroundings of our age to realize how severe was the struggle for existence of primitive man in America—what the condition of the Indian was in the days before the white man had come, bringing with him firearms which kill at a distance and horses which can overtake the buffalo. To comprehend this, we must stop and think, try to imagine conditions some centuries back in the time of the stone age, when the people, wholly without knowledge of metal, slew the wild beasts on which they subsisted with weapons made of flint, and moved from place to place on foot, carrying all they owned on their backs or on the dog travois.

In those days the securing of daily food must have been a difficult matter for many tribes, and the laying up of any provision for the future doubly hard. The great beasts, so easily slaughtered by the rifle, or even by the iron-headed arrow shot into them at a close range by a mounted man, must have been nearly invulnerable to the stone-headed arrow. The tough thick hide, covered with a close mat of fur, presents resistance to the keen edge of even a modern knife and could have been pierced only by the best arrows of that day, shot at very short range; and if the careful hunter crept close enough to the buffalo, and his arm was strong enough to drive the blunt-headed shaft deep into the body, the great beast, irritated, instead of running away, might turn and fight the one who had injured it. Often, no doubt, the man kept out of sight and shot arrow after arrow into it, for there was no sound to alarm it, and the buffalo could not tell from where the hurt came; but let the animal learn the cause of this pain, and the man was in great danger. A wounded buffalo was a terrible antagonist, swift of foot, resistless in power, only to be avoided by the exercise of cunning and speed. In the age of stone the contest between wild man and wild beast was not an unequal one. The animal was the stronger, the quicker, and the better armed of the two. Man's advantage lay altogether in his intelligence.

Echoes of the fear in which these huge animals were held may still be discovered in the traditional stories of certain tribes, which told how, in those days, the buffalo used to chase, kill, and eat the people. Such tales, still given with considerable detail among the Blackfeet, the Arikaras, and other tribes, relate how greatly the buffalo were dreaded in ancient times. Such fear could hardly have arisen except as the result of actual experience of their power to inflict injury and death.

Since the effort to secure it was often attended with so much danger, it must have occurred to the early hunters to devise some method for capturing food in quantity that was more certain and more safe than the spear and the bow and arrow alone. The first steps toward solving it involved improving the traps and snares which were employed for the capture of the smaller animals and the evolution of the pen with extended wings, into which the buffalo or antelope were lured and chased and captured whole herds at a time. In those early days, the hunter closely studied the animals among which he lived. He was constantly engaged in watching them and trying to learn how they would act under particular conditions. Long before the traps were devised he must have known of the existence in buffalo, elk, and antelope of that curiosity which made the trap feasible, and which to the animals proved so self-destructive.

Today you can see, scattered along the flanks of the Rocky Mountains and at many points of the great central plateau, the remains of the ancient traps in which the these long-ago hunters once took the buffalo. Most of the tribes gave up their use many years ago—after they obtained horses—and the more perishable portions of wings and enclosures have long since crumbled to decay; but in various locations in Montana and Colorado, the plains are still marked by the long lines of heaped-up stones which formed the arms of the chute that guided the doomed animals toward the cliff or the slaughter pen.

The common method of taking buffalo, by those tribes which inhabited the broken country close to the mountains, was to build a V-shaped chute, the arms of which extended far out on the prairie and came together at the top of a cliff, or a cut bank, over which the buffalo were expected to fall. If the cliff was high

and vertical, the fall killed or crippled many of the animals, but if it was only a cut bank of moderate height, an enclosure was built at the foot of the bank below the angle of the V, from which the animals could not escape after they had made the plunge. We may imagine that originally they attempted to drive the buffalo over high cliffs, where the fall would kill them, and that the enclosure was a later development from this.

The building of one of these traps involved a great deal of labor and so took a long time, but after it had been completed, it was practically indestructible, and with annual repairs would last for generations.

Buffalo Hunt on Horseback

In the 1800s a traveler described the buffalo hunt.

"News of the buffalo approaching an Indian camp is received several days before the animals appear, as they only move forward when the grazing is not sufficient. Where a large camp is stationed they usually hunt by 'surround,' which is as follows:

"The hunters hold a council with the chief in the hunters' lodge and prohibit any individual hunting ahead of the buffalo, they also send runners daily on discovery, to observe what progress they are making toward the camp, their numbers, etc. When they report them to be near enough another meeting is held in the lodge, the time for the hunt appointed, and notice given to the camp by the haranguing of the public crier. At daybreak all the horses are caught and saddled, and each of the horsemen is provided with a bow and a quiver of arrows. A number who have no horses arm themselves with guns, and at a signal from one of the hunters the party moves off in single file or line. Those who have the fastest horses go in front, and after them come the other horsemen. Then come the foot hunters, and lastly the women with their dogs and travois. The soldiers ride along each side the line (which is sometimes a mile and more in length) and observe whether the line of march is preserved, and that no one leaves singly. Were a dog to run out of the line it would be shot with an arrow immediately.

"Their march is conducted in silence, with the wind in their faces, consequently blowing the scent away from the buffalo while they are coming near them. The animal is not quick sighted but very keen scented, and a man can, in passing across the wind blowing toward them, raise a herd at the distance of two or three miles, without their seeing him.

"The party proceeds in this order, taking every advantage of concealment the country affords in hills, bushes, long grass, etc., endeavoring to get around the herd. As soon, however, as they are close and see a movement among the buffalo intimating flight, they push their horses at full speed, and riding entirely around, commence shooting the buffalo, which run in the direction of the footmen, these in their turn shoot, and the animals are driven back toward the horses. In this way they are kept running nearly in a circle until very tired, and the greater part are killed. Those on horseback shoot arrows into all they can at the distance of from two to six paces, and the footmen load and fire as often as the animals come near them.

"A 'surround' party of eighty to one hundred persons will in this way kill from one hundred to five hundred buffalo in the course of an hour.

"As soon as possible the women get to work skinning and cutting up the animals. The tongue, hide, and four best pieces are the property of the one who killed it, and the rest belongs to those who skin it. When the men have stopped killing and turned their horses loose to graze they commence with their women, and the work being divided among so many is soon gotten through with. If any disputes occur as to the right to the hides or meat, they are settled on the spot by the hunters; but these disputes do not often occur, as they generally all have as many hides and as much meat as they can pack home. The meat is cut in long, thick slices, merely detaching it from the bones, and leaving the carcass on the plains. It is packed home on their horses and dogs. Before leaving, however, they all make a hearty meal of raw liver, raw kidneys, raw stomach, and cow's nose, with other parts in the same state, and the blood being thus smeared over all their faces presents a savage appearance.

"On arrival in camp, if the hunters wish the tongues, each one throws his down at the lodge in passing, or sends it to them. Each also furnishes a piece of meat for that lodge. All the old and feeble are supplied by their relatives who have been to the hunt. The chief has no voice in all these matters. He sometimes hunts and works the same as the others, but generally sends some of his sons or other relations with his horses for meat. They never use the gun on horseback or the bow on foot after game. The former they cannot load while running and the latter is not calculated to shoot with certainty any distance over ten paces."

The Buffalo Trap

This is the most ancient mode of hunting, and probably the most successful one prior to the introduction of firearms and horses, as their bows and arrows are insufficient for killing buffalo on foot.

When a camp of thirty to sixty lodges finds itself without guns and horses, they move to a suitable place to build a park and there wait the approach of buffalo toward it. Most streams have high bluffs on each side and a valley between. They therefore pitch their camp in the valley opposite and near a gap of perpendicular descent through the hills; a high level plain being beyond the bluffs. They cut timber and plant strong posts in the ground nearly in a circular form and fill up the openings between with large logs, rocks, bushes, and everything that will in any way add to its strength, inclosing an area of nearly an acre of ground. This enclosure is run up the sides of the hill to the gap or entrance, though neither it nor the camp is visible from the place beyond. The whole is planned and managed by the master of the park, some divining man of

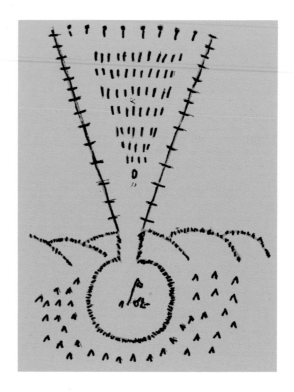

known repute, who is believed to have the power of making the buffalo come into it by his enchantments.

On the plains beyond, and commencing where the wood mark leaves off, are thrown up piles of earth, about three feet high and large enough to conceal a man lying behind them, which are about eighteen paces apart and extend in angles to the distance of a quarter to half a mile in proportion as there are people to man them. When these arrangements are completed, four fast-running young men are selected by the manager whose duty it is to scour the country every day or two, making a circuit of about twenty miles in discovery of buffalo, and report to headquarters. The master in the meantime commences his magic arts as follows: A flag-staff or pole is planted in the center of the park, to the top of which is attached a yard or two of scarlet cloth, some tobacco, and a cow's horn. This is a sacrifice to the Wind.

At the foot of the same are placed two or three buffalo heads, which are painted red and decked out in feathers, and new kettles with scarlet cloth and other things are placed before them. These are given to the Buffalo Spirits.

Another head painted and decked very gaudily is placed in the lodge of the master, who smokes and invokes it, at times singing the Bull Song, which he accompanies with a rattle nearly all night, and prophesies as to their appearance of success in the morning. A man is now chosen who is to lead the buffalo within the lines, and there are but few among them who can do it. When the discoverers have reported buffalo to be within eight or ten miles of the camp, and the wind is favorable, the master, after great ceremonies to the heads, and making them other sacrifices, gives notice that a throw must be made, sending all the camp to take their stations behind the piles of earth, lying down; he remains in camp, keeping up a singing, rattling, and smoking—with invocations all the time. The person who brings the buffalo mounts a horse and meets them a great distance from camp. When within about a hundred and fifty yards of the herd he covers his body with his robe, lies along the horse's back, and imitates the bleating of a buffalo calf.

The whole mass immediately moves toward him. He retreats toward the pen, always keeping to the windward of them, and about the same distance ahead, renewing the noise of the calf whenever they appear to stop. They generally follow him as fast as his horse can gallop, and in this way alone he conducts them within the lines of the angle. Of course as soon as they are a short distance in, the scent of one of the angles reaches them but it is now too late, they have closed in behind. The animals now take fright and rush from one line to another, but seeing people on both sides (who rise as the buffalo attempt to get through) they keep straight forward. The leader on horseback now makes his escape to one side, and the whole herd plunges madly down the precipice, one on top of the other, breaking their legs and necks in the fall. Into the pen they tumble, those in front having no power to stop. They are forced on by the pressure from behind and frightened by the yelling and firing of the hunters.

When all have passed into the pen the work of slaughter commences, with guns and bows firing as long as any appearance of life remains. From three hundred to six hundred are thus thrown in at one time by a small camp, and two or three days are required to skin and cut them up.

Men, women, and children now commence skinning. Each secures as many hides as he can skin. The
master of the park claims a portion for his share,
indeed all are said to belong to him, but he does not
take more than the rest. All the tongues, however, are
his, and he also receives other payment for his services
in presents, besides the standing of a divining man.

Stalking the Buffalo

This is done on foot with a bow and arrow or with a
gun by a single man. It is indispensable he should have
on a skin dress in summer and a white blanket coat
over it in winter, or a buffalo robe coat with all the hair
turned inside.

Any dark-colored dress is easily seen by the animals
at a considerable distance, but white or light-colored
clothing does not attract their notice. If the hunter is
using a gun, he covers it with skin to prevent the dirt
or snow from entering the barrel while in the act of
crawling. His accoutrements are also firmly attached
to his person by a belt. He proceeds toward the buffalo, keeping the wind as nearly in his face as possible,
sometimes being obliged to make a circuit of miles to
get the wind in the right direction. When near the animals, he observes from the top of some hill how they

are stationed, which way they travel, and the nature of the ground as regards coulees, gullies, bushes, grass, and any objects that may hide his person from their view and shapes his course according to the means of concealment presented. If he finds the country too level to get them within range, he then commences crawling on his belly toward them.

This is a very laborious and slow mode of progressing and often takes one or two hours to come within shooting distance, as the hunter only moves while the animals are eating, stopping the moment their attention is directed toward him. In the snow it is a very cold business, and in the summer difficult on account of the cactus, but they are obliged to do it frequently in both seasons on these level plains. Great precaution is needed to approach buffalo or antelope on a level plain. The hunter sometimes covers his head with sage bushes, and sticks the same or grass in his belt; at other times a wolf skin covers his head and back— he lying flat, no form of the man can be perceived— and the animals being accustomed to these objects do not affright so easily. When by any of these means he has arrived within shooting distance he fires without rising, elevating his gun by support of the elbows, or rises slowly in order to take his shot with his bow and arrow. After shooting he remains motionless a few minutes during which the buffalo, after recoiling a few paces, and seeing nothing on the move, commence grazing. He now turns over on his back and reloads his gun (lying in this position) by putting the butt against his foot—and when ready will turn over on his belly and fire again, and so on, sometimes killing six or eight without changing his place, or with very little movement.

Once he rises the herd runs off and he commences skinning. Some hunters mimic the bleating of a calf and thus decoy the buffalo to them, but this is a rare talent, and only practiced by a few good performers; in hilly places or where there are gullies and bushes to hide the hunter, neither buffalo nor antelope are difficult to kill, but on the barren and level plain it requires great exertion, time, and patience.

THE WINTER HUNT

Another method by which great numbers of both buffalo and antelope are taken is when the snow has drifted in the gullies, forming banks ten to fifteen feet deep. The animals are chased into the drifts on foot. The hunter goes over the snow on snowshoes, but the animals become embedded and are killed with ease. In the summer when several animals are killed, the meat is placed in a pile covered with the hides, and a portion of the hunter's clothing left on it, the scent of which prevents the foxes and the wolves from coming to it.

In the winter the usual way is to bury the meat in the snow, which effectually prevents the scavengers from finding it, as they have little ability to smell through several feet of snow. Meat can be left in this way in perfect security for a month or more, but ordinarily they return with their dogs and take it away the next day.

Antelope were hunted in the same way, also sometimes decoyed by tying some portion of clothing to a pole, the man lying down and raising and lowering the pole at intervals, or by kicking up his heels, one after the other. They have great curiosity to see the strange object, and after making many circles will come near enough to get a shot, though as soon as they make out the man they are off. A wolf skin was said to be the best disguise when hunting animals on foot.

DEER HUNTING

Deer hunting involved: finding the deer, approaching it, shooting it, cutting it up, and carrying it home. Deer are hunted in timber by a man alone and on foot. He must be well acquainted with the habits of the animal, where it is to be found at different hours in the day, what it feeds upon at different seasons, to know by the tracks if it is traveling, grazing, running, retiring to rest, or going to water; he must be quick sighted, a good walker, and go cautiously through the bush when near the game. The morning and evening are the best times to hunt them, as they are then on the edge or borders of the woods where grass is found or in open places in the bottoms; returning into the thick bushes for a few hours in the middle of the day. The hunter travels fast until he comes near the place where he judges a deer is to be found, then proceeds very slowly and silently, looking in every direction, always keeping the wind in his favor until the animal is seen. He then approaches it stepping from tree to tree, bush to bush, crawling and creeping, hiding himself entirely from its view, by every means, and making no noise. When he thinks he is within range he rises and fires quickly and the deer falls. It is then skinned and cut up, the meat packed in the hide and tied in a bundle by the skin of the legs, in such a way as to form a collar, which is drawn over his forehead by lying or sitting down and slipping it over, then rising up with the weight between his shoulders he starts homeward. If more than one is wanted he caches the first on a tree after cutting up, and proceeds in quest of others, sometimes killing three or four in a day, which he returns for with his horse or dogs the next day.

ELK HUNTING

This was done on foot but by parties of men. Elk travel in large droves and are found in the large timbered bottoms of the Missouri and Yellowstone. There was some ceremony required in hunting this animal. In the first place some divining woman who is said to be an "elk dreamer" declares that she has had a favorable dream for hunting them. The woman is then stripped to the waist and also barelegged, the body and face painted a bright yellow, and a wreath of bushes with leaves on projecting two or three feet on each side is placed on her head in imitation of the horns of the elk. Thus decorated she starts at the head of a party of men. When in the vicinity of the place where, according to her dream, the elk are to be found, she stops and begins her song, while the others continue in quest of the game. As soon as the herd is discovered the party separates and—outflanking them on either side—commences running toward them, shouting while running. When the elk become confused, they scatter and turn in different directions, presenting marks for the various hunters.

They were then skinned, cut up, and the meat and hides packed home. The skins are used for clothing and the meat, though eaten, was not a favored dish of the Native Americans.

Elk are also approached singly, and at those times the same precautions are used as when deer hunting, though elk are not as shy and timid an animal as deer.

HUNTING THE GRIZZLY BEAR

This animal was not often hunted, but often found when not desired, and mostly passed by unmolested by the single Indian, though on occasions they did kill them when they met. This was an exploit that ranked in bravery next to killing an enemy, but the thickets they inhabit made the pursuit too dangerous for ordinary hunters. They are more frequently killed in their dens in winter.

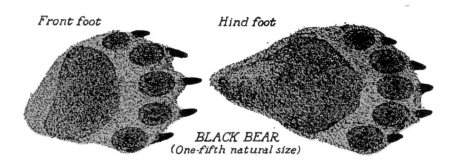

Front foot Hind foot

BLACK BEAR
(One-fifth natural size)

The grizzly bear in the beginning of cold weather and snow seeks some hole in the side of a hill in some solitary place, and carries in a quantity of grass and brush to make his nest. There he lies all winter asleep and eats nothing, though they are said to derive some nourishment by sucking their paws. The nest or wash is always within a few feet of the entrance and they can easily be seen from the outside. Generally a den contains two to four bears, or one large male and two yearling cubs, or one large female and two yearlings. Sometimes, however, they are found singly. When a den is discovered, six or eight hunters lay siege to it, approaching the hole close enough to see the foremost bear. Then three of them shoot, the others reserving their arrows. They all run off some distance and if the animal pursues them, the rest loose their shots. If the first one has been killed and there are others in the den, the hunters light a fire at the entrance to smoke them out. If none appear, they conclude there is only one, enter, and drag him out.

Frequently two or three bears are killed in the same hole at the same time, and at others some of the hunters get dreadfully mangled. Bears were also run on horseback, when found on the plains, and shot with arrows. This is the least dangerous manner of killing them.

Pits or traps are not generally used, though occasionally forked sticks are placed in the entrance to the hole so that when the bear came out he was caught by the hind part and detained a short time.

When a bear is killed he is skinned, all except the head, which is covered with scarlet cloth, the hair smeared over with vermilion, handsome feathers stuck around it, and new kettles and tobacco laid before it. It is presented with the pipe to smoke and a long ceremony of invocation takes place, praying that his spirit may have pity upon their wives and children and not tear them when they are hunting after fruit and berries. They say if this is not done the bear will surely sooner or later devour some of them or their children.

BEAVER

The beaver was hunted throughout the temperate wetlands of North America, but until the Europeans introduced steel traps, it was not often trapped. Instead, parties of young hunters—usually boys—worked the dens with long sticks to dislodge the animals, clubbing them when they appeared.

BUTCHERING THE BUFFALO

The Native Americans were expert butchers, and it did not take long for them to skin the buffalo. The hide was drawn to one side, and the meat was rapidly cut from the bones; then the visceral cavity was opened, the long intestine taken out, emptied of its contents, and rolled up. Then the paunch was opened, emptied, and put aside with the liver and heart. The skull was broken and the brains removed. The tongue was saved. Very likely the liver was cut up on the spot and was eaten raw. Women and children tore off and eagerly devoured lumps of the sweet white fat that clings to the outside of the intestine. All were cheerful, though hard at work, as the children played merrily about. The camp dogs gorged themselves on the rejected portions and gnawed at the stripped skeletons. When work on a buffalo was finished, the hide, hair side down, was thrown on a horse or travois, and on this the meat was packed. The ends of the hide were then turned up, and the whole was lashed in place with lariats. Then the party moved on to look for another buffalo killed by an arrow belonging to their lodge, or began the trip back to their village or camp.

On reaching camp, the loads were taken off, the hides were folded up, and most of the meat was cut into thin strips and hung on the drying scaffolds. When this had been done the hides were spread out on the ground, and the women, armed with fleshers of stone or bone, begin to cleanse them of all the flesh, fat, and blood that clings to them.

DRESSING HIDES

To make a robe, the hide of the buffalo was taken off in two halves by slitting the animal down the middle of the back and the middle of the belly. Afterward, the portions of meat and membrane adhering to it were removed, so that it will present a smooth clear skin.

This was done with a tool made from the shin bone of an elk. The skin was then hung up at one corner on a pole and the meat was dug off by a downward hoeing action of the implement. A woman might finish this operation on two whole skins—or four halves—in one day.

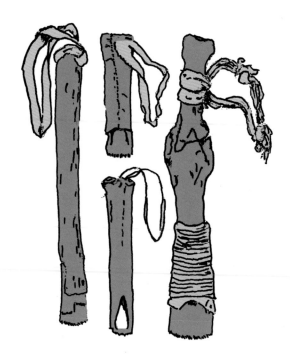

Next the skin was stretched to dry. Holes were cut through it near the edge. In summer it was pinned to the ground by wooden pegs; in winter, when the ground was frozen, it was stretched on a frame of four poles lashed together, with a small fire built to dry it. When dry, the next thing to be done was to scrape it, that is, to hoe off about one third of the thickness of the hide. This was done with a flint tool, which was held in both hands. The hide was then laid on the ground, and the woman standing on it, stooping, dug off the hide in shavings until it was of the proper thickness.

This occupied about half a day to each whole hide and was a very tiring work. Grease was then melted and sprinkled sparingly over the skin. Then it was suspended over a small fire for a few hours so that the grease might penetrate it. Afterward it was taken down and smeared over with the brains or livers of some animals that had been boiled in water, soaking it thoroughly, and then left all night in this state. In the morning it was again stretched on the frame, the liver scraped off, clean water thrown on, and scraped off until the hide became white. A fire was then made nearby and the skin was slowly heated and rubbed with pumice stone or porous bone until it was about half dry. Then it was taken out of the frame and pulled backward and forward round a strong cord of sinew that was tied at each end to the lodge pole. Every few minutes the skin was held a short time to the fire, then rubbed, and this operation continued until it became perfectly dry and soft. This was also hard work. A good hand will rub two whole skins or four halves in a day. The skin was now dressed. The holes made for stretching it around the edges were cut off and it was sewed

up along the back with an awl and sinew, which took about half an hour for each two halves of the buffalo.

Deer and elk skins underwent the same operations, though they were skinned whole and not in halves like the buffalo hides. It is clear that at least three days are required to dress one buffalo robe. Twenty-five to thirty-five robes was considered an excellent winter's work for one woman.

Wolf, bear, fox, rabbit, beaver, hare, ermine, lynx, otter, rat, mink, etc. were skinned, stretched, and dried by the men and boys. A wolf or fox skin was now and then dressed for the use of a woman or hunter to wear round his head, and underwent the preceding operations, though the skin being small and light, not much labor was required.

CHAPTER SEVEN: NATIVE AMERICAN DIET

For the Native peoples of North America, there was very little trade in food, and the specifics of any diet depended on the availability of the particular plants and animals in the region in which they lived. But we can make a few generalizations.

PROTEIN

People along the eastern seacoast ate fish, mussels, clams, and waterfowl. A little inland they depended on venison, all manner of birds, and the smaller mammals like rabbit, squirrel, and possum. The people living on the Great Plains and in the Great Basin, all the way to the eastern foothills of the Rockies, were a buffalo culture. In the far north, Caribou, fish, and seal made up the bulk of the protein diet. The people living on the Northwest Coast took fish and whales from the sea and salmon from the rivers and streams.

AGRICULTURE

The practice of settled agriculture, the archeologists tell us, came comparatively late to North America, but by Contact it was well established, especially in the East and in the Southwest where the staple crops included maize, beans, and squash.

GATHERING

All North Americans supplemented whatever they hunted and farmed by gathering the foods that grew wild all around them.

Wild rice grew throughout the interior wetlands and in the lakes and tributaries of the great rivers.

We can get a good idea of the sheer variety of berries, roots, and other vegetables eaten by hunter-gatherers like the Assiniboine people of the Upper Missouri River region in the following table.

English Name	Assiniboine name	Preparation
Prairie turnip (*pomme blanche*)	*Teep-se-nah*	Dried and pounded
Service berries	*We-pah-zoo-kah*	Dried
Bull berries (*grains des boeufs*)	*Taque-sha-shah*	Dried
Chokecherries	*Cham-pah*	Pounded with seeds and dried

English Name	Assiniboine name	Preparation
Red plums	*Caun-tah*	Stones extracted and dried
Wild grapes	*Chint-kah*	Not preserved; eaten ripe
Currants	*Wecha-ge-nus-kah*	Eaten ripe
Gooseberries	*Chap-tah-ha-zah*	Eaten ripe
Wild rhubarb	*Chan-hn-no-ha*	Tops eaten raw or boiled
Fungus growing on trees	*Chaun-no-ghai*	Not dried; found in winter
Artichokes	*Pung-ghai*	Eaten raw or boiled; not preserved
Berries of the red willow	*Chau-sha-sha*	Eaten raw only in great need
Antelope turnips	*Ta-to-ka-na Teep-se-nah*	Boiled and dried
Wild garlic	*Ta-poo-zint-kah*	Raw; not preserved
A berry called	*Me-nun*	Not dried; eaten ripe
Acorns	*Ou-tah-pe*	Roasted and dried
Strawberries	*Wa-zshu-sta-cha*	Not dried
Inner bark of cottonwood	*Wah-chin-cha-ha*	Resorted to in time of actual famine
Berries of the smoking weed	*She-o-tak-kah*	Not preserved; eaten ripe
A root resembling artichoke	*Ske-ske-chah*	Dried, pounded, and boiled
Buds of the wild rose	*We-ze-zeet-kah*	Found everywhere all winter on the stalk
Red haw berries	*Tas-paun*	Not dried; eaten in fall and winter

CAMAS OR WILD HYACINTH

The bulbs were gathered in the late summer or fall, after the leaves had withered. The bulbs were roasted in fire pits and tasted something like sweet potatoes, or they were dried and pounded into a flour to make a kind of bread.

In many places along the flanks of the mountains the *camas* root grew in such abundance that it formed an important item in the subsistence of some tribes. After being dug by the women, it was subjected to a cooking process before being dried. A large pit was dug, in which a fire was built and kept burning until the earth at the bottom and sides of the pit was thoroughly heated. Then the ashes were removed, and the pit lined with grass and filled with camas roots. More grass was then laid on top with roots and a little earth on the grass; a hot fire was built on top of the whole, which burned until the mass was cooked. This process of cooking distilled a brown sweet syrupy fluid, which was eagerly sought for by the children, who greedily sucked the grass with which the pit was lined. After the bulbs had been cooked, they were removed from the pit, spread out in the sun to dry, and afterward stowed in baskets or sacks.

BERRIES

In the various seasons when the different berries ripened, the branches of the shrubs were torn off and beaten over a robe spread on the ground. Then they were dried in the sun and stored for winter use. Sometimes, before they were thoroughly dry, they were pressed together into cakes—to be eaten like a bread with meat—but more often the dried fruit was stewed and eaten with boiled dried meat. The fruit of the wild cherry was pounded to crush the seed and then dried.

DIGGING STICK

For collecting roots they provided themselves with a stick about three feet long, curved, and sharpened at the point, shaped somewhat like a sacking needle. This was used to unearth the roots.

PLANTING STICK

The planting stick was much the same tool as the digging stick, except that it was often shovel-shaped at its point.

TREE NUTS

Mast, or the fruit of the beech, oak, chestnut, walnut, hickory nut, and other trees, and along with maize, provided the basic breadstuff of Native peoples of North America. The nuts were gathered in the fall, dried to prevent sprouting, and cached. Later the dried nuts were pounded into a flour for thickening stews; or mixed with water or animal fat and baked into a kind of bread.

The hickory nut was mashed, boiled, and strained to make a sweet milk-like drink. Other nuts were pressed for their oil.

The people of the Great Basin harvested piñon nuts. The cones were roasted in large pits, pounded to separate the seed from the cone, roasted again, pulped, and mixed with water to form a thickish gruel. A great favorite.

BARK

Often the people of the mountain tribes peeled the bark from certain trees at the proper season of the year and gathered the soft sweet inner coating that lies next to the wood. Some tribes, like the Kutenais and Flatheads, collected spruce gum and chewed it.

A SIT-DOWN DINNER

Adapted from reports by George Catlin from his travels among the Indigenous peoples of North America in the early 1800s.

The Mandans are somewhat of agriculturists, as they raise a great deal of corn and some pumpkins and squash. This is all done by the women, who make their hoes from the shoulder-blade of the buffalo or the elk, and dig the ground over, piling it into mounds instead of plowing it. They raise a very small sort of corn, the ears of which are not longer than a man's thumb. This variety is well adapted to their climate, as it ripens sooner than other varieties, which would not mature in so cold a latitude. The green corn season is one of great festivity with them, and one of much importance. The greater part of their crop is eaten during these festivals, and the remainder is gathered and dried on the cob, before it has ripened, and packed away in "caches" (as the French call them), holes dug in the ground, some six or seven feet deep, the insides of which are somewhat in the form of a jug, and tightly closed at the top. The corn, and even dried meat and pemmican, are placed in these caches, packed tight around the sides, with prairie grass. This preserved it through the severest winters.

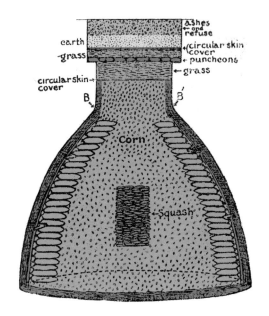

FOOD PRESERVATION

Corn and dried meat are generally laid in the fall, in sufficient quantities to support the village through the winter. In addition, they often store great quantities of dried squashes and dried turnips that grow in great abundance in these regions. These are dried in great quantities, pounded into a sort of meal, and cooked with the dried meat and corn. Wild fruit of different kinds are also dried and laid up for the winter season, such as buffalo berries, service berries, strawberries, and wild plums.

The buffalo meat, however, is the great staple and "staff of life" in this country, and seldom fails to afford them an abundant and wholesome means of subsistence. During the summer and fall months they use the meat fresh, and cook it in a great variety of ways, by roasting, broiling, boiling, stewing, smoking, etc. By boiling the ribs and joints with the marrow in them, they make a delicious soup, which is eaten in vast quantities. The Mandan, I find, have no regular or stated times for their meals, but generally eat about twice in the twenty-four hours. The pot is always boiling over the fire, and anyone who is hungry (either of the household or from any other part of the village) has a right to order it taken off, and to fall to eating as he pleases.

THE RIGHT TO EAT

Such is an unvarying custom amongst the North American Indians, and I very much doubt whether the civilized world have in their institutions any system which can properly be called more humane and charitable. Every man, woman, or child in Indian communities is allowed to enter any one's lodge, even that of the chief of the nation, and eat when they are hungry, provided misfortune or necessity has driven them to it. Even the poorest and most worthless drone of the nation, if he is too lazy to hunt or to supply himself, can walk into any lodge and everyone will share with him as long as there is anything to eat. He, however, who thus begs when he is able to hunt, pays dear for his meat, for he is stigmatized with the disgraceful epithet of a beggar.

The Mandans, like all other tribes, sit at their meals cross-legged, or rather with their ankles crossed in front of them, and both feet drawn close under their bodies; or, which is very often the case also, they take their meals in a reclining posture, with the legs thrown out, and the body resting on one elbow and fore-arm, which are under them. The dishes from which they eat are invariably on the ground or floor of the lodge, and the group resting on buffalo robes or mats.

The position in which the women sit at their meals and on other occasions is different from that of the men, and one which they take and rise from again, with great ease and much grace. By merely bending the knees both together and inclining the body back and the head and shoulders quite forward, they squat entirely down to the ground, inclining both feet either to the right or the left. In this position they always rest while eating, and it is both modest and graceful, for they seem, with apparent ease, to assume the position and rise out of it, without using their hands in any way to assist them.

These women, however, although graceful and civil, and ever so beautiful or ever so hungry, are not allowed to sit in the same group with the men while at their meals. So far as I have yet traveled in the Indian country, I never have seen an Indian woman eating with her husband. Men form the first group at the banquet, and women and children and dogs all come together at the next, and these gormandize and glut themselves to an enormous extent, though the men very seldom do.

It is time that an error on this subject, which has gone generally abroad in the world, was corrected. It is everywhere asserted, and almost universally believed, that the Indians are "enormous eaters." But comparatively speaking, I assure my readers that this is an error. I venture to say that there are no persons on earth who practice greater prudence and self-denial than the men do (amongst the wild Indians), who are constantly in war and in the chase, or in their athletic sports and exercises; for all of which they are excited by the highest ideas of pride and honor, and every kind of excess is studiously avoided; and for a very great part of their lives, the most painful abstinence is enforced upon themselves, for the purpose of preparing their bodies and their limbs for these extravagant exertions.

These men generally eat but twice a day, and many times not more than once, and those meals are light and simple compared with the meals that are swallowed in the civilized world—and by the very people also who sit at the festive board three times a day, making a jest of the Indian for his eating, when they actually guzzle more liquids, besides their eating, than would fill the stomach of an Indian.

There are, however, many seasons and occasions in the year with all Indians, when they fast for several days in succession; and others where they can get nothing to eat; and at such times (their habits are such) they may be seen to commence with an enormous meal, and because they do so it is an insufficient reason why we should forever remain under so egregious an error with regard to a single custom of these people. I have seen so many of these, and lived with them, and traveled with them, and oftentimes felt as if I should starve to death on an equal allowance, that I am fully convinced I am correct in saying that the North American Indians, taking them in the aggregate, even where they have an abundance to subsist on, eat less than any civilized population of equal numbers that I have ever traveled amongst.

CURING MEAT

Their mode of curing and preserving the buffalo meat is somewhat curious, and in fact it is almost incredible, for it is all cured or dried in the sun, without the aid of salt or smoke! The method of doing this is the same amongst all the tribes, and is as follows:

The choicest parts of the flesh from the buffalo are cut out by the squaws, carried home on their backs or on horses, and there cut "across the grain," in such a manner as will take alternately the layers of lean and fat; and having prepared it all in this way, in strips about half an inch in thickness, it is hung up by the hundreds and thousands of pounds on poles resting on crotches, out of the reach of dogs or wolves, and exposed to the rays of the sun for several days, when it becomes so effectually dried, that it can be carried to any part of the world without damage. This seems almost an unaccountable thing, and the more so, as it is done in the hottest months of the year and also in all the different latitudes.

So singular a fact as this can only be accounted for, I consider, on the ground of the extraordinary rarity and purity of the air which we meet with in these vast tracts of country, which are now properly denominated "the

great buffalo plains," a series of exceedingly elevated plateaus of steppes or prairies, lying at and near the base of the Rocky Mountains.

NO-SALT DIET

It is a fact then, which I presume will be new to most of the world, that meat can be cured in the sun without the aid of smoke or salt; and it is a fact equally true and equally surprising that none of these tribes use salt in any way, although their country abounds in salt springs; and in many places, in the frequent walks of the Indian, the prairie may be seen, for miles together, covered with an incrustation of salt as white as the drifted snow.

I have, in traveling with Indians, encamped by such places, where they have cooked and eaten their meat, when I have been unable to prevail on them to use salt in any quantity whatever. The Indians cook their meat more than the civilized people do, and I have long since learned, from necessity, that meat thus cooked can easily be eaten and relished too, without salt or other condiment.

FEAST

The simple feast which was spread before us consisted of three dishes only, two of which were served in wooden bowls, and the third in an earthen vessel of their own manufacture, somewhat in shape of a bread-tray in our own country. This last contained a quantity of pemmican and marrow fat, and one of the former held a fine brace of buffalo ribs, delightfully roasted; the other was filled with a kind of paste or pudding, made of the flour of the *pomme blanche*, as the French call it, a delicious turnip of the prairie, finely flavored with the buffalo berries, which are collected in great quantities in this country and used with diverse dishes in cooking, as we in civilized countries use dried currants, which they very much resemble.

A handsome pipe and a tobacco pouch made of the otter skin, filed with *k'nick-k'neck* (Indian tobacco), laid by the side of the feast. When we were stated, mine host took up his pipe and deliberately filled it; and instead of lighting it by the fire, which he could easily, he drew from his pouch his flint and steel, and so raised a spark, drew a few strong whiffs through it, and presented to my mouth, through which I drew a whiff or two while he held it in his hands. This done, he laid down the pipe and, drawing his knife from his belt, cut off a very small piece of the meat from the ribs, and pronouncing these words: "*Ho-pe-ne-chee wa-pa-shee*" (meaning a medicine sacrifice), threw it into the fire.

He then (by signals) requested me to eat, and I commenced, after drawing out from my belt my knife (which it is supposed that every man in this country carries about him, for at an Indian feast a knife is never offered to a guest). Reader, be not astonished that I sat and ate my dinner alone, for such is the custom of this strange land. In all tribes in these western regions it is an invariable rule that a chief never eats with the guests invited to a feast; but while they eat, he sits by at their service, ready to wait upon them, deliberately charging and lighting the pipe, which is to be passed around after the feast is over.

Such was the case in the present instance, and while I was eating, Mih-to-toh-pa sat cross-legged before me, cleaning his pipe and preparing it for a cheerful smoke when I had finished my meal. For this ceremony

I observed he was making unusual preparation, and I observed as I ate, that after he had taken enough of the *k'nick-k'neck*, or bark of the red willow, from his pouch, he rolled out of it also a piece of the "castor," which it is customary amongst these folks to carry in their tobacco sack to give it a flavor; and, shaving off a small quantity of it, he mixed it with the bark, with which he charged his pipe.

This done, he drew also from his sack a small parcel containing a fine powder, which was made of dried buffalo dung, a little of which he spread over the top—according also to custom—which was like tinder, having no other effect than that of lighting the pipe, with ease and satisfaction. My appetite satiated, I straightened up and with a whiff the pipe was lit, and we enjoyed together for a quarter of an hour the most delightful exchange of good feelings, amid clouds of smoke and pantomimic signs and gesticulations.

PEMMICAN

The dish of pemmican and marrow fat, of which I spoke, was an article of food used throughout this country, as familiarly as we use bread in the civilized world. It is made of buffalo meat dried very hard and afterwards pounded in a large wooden mortar until it is made nearly as fine as sawdust. It is then packed in this dry state in bladders or sacks of skin and is easily carried to any part of the world in good order. Marrow fat is collected by the Indians from the buffalo bones which they break to pieces, yielding a prodigious quantity of marrow, which is boiled out and put into buffalo bladders which have been distended; and after it cools, it becomes quite hard, like tallow, and has the appearance, and very nearly the flavor, of the richest yellow butter. At a feast, chunks of this marrow fat are cut off and placed in a tray or bowl with the pemmican, and eaten together, which we civilized folks in these regions consider a very good substitute for bread and butter. In this dish laid a spoon made of the buffalo's horn, which was black as jet and beautifully polished; in one of the others there was another of still more ingenious and beautiful workmanship, made of the horn of the mountain sheep, or *Gros corn* as the French trappers call them; it was large enough to hold of itself two or three pints and was almost entirely transparent.

I spoke also of the earthen dishes or bowls in which these viands were served out; they are a familiar part of the culinary furniture of every Mandan lodge. Manufactured by the women of this tribe in great quantities, they are modeled into a thousand forms and tastes. They are made by the hands of the women, from a tough black clay, and baked in kilns which are made for the purpose and are nearly equal in hardness to our own manufacture of pottery—though they have not yet got the art of glazing, which would be to them a most valuable secret. They make them so strong and serviceable, however, that they hang them over the fire as we do our iron pots, and boil their meat in them with perfect success.

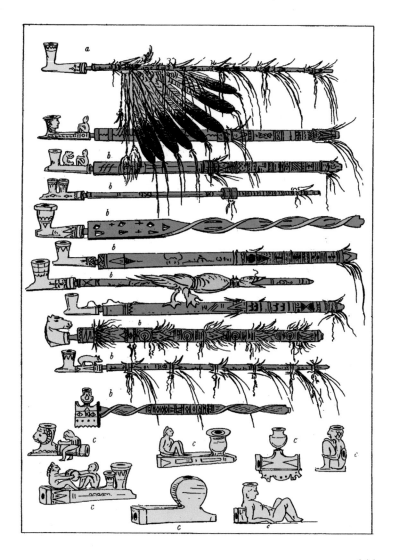

Whilst sitting at this feast the wigwam was as silent as death, although we were not alone in it. This chief, like most others, had a plurality of wives, and all of them (some six or seven) were seated around the sides of the lodge, upon robes or mats placed upon the ground, and were not allowed to speak, though they were in readiness to obey his orders or commands, which were uniformly given by signs manual and were executed in the neatest and most silent manner.

CHAPTER EIGHT: CLOTHING

ROBES

The typical robe was made of the skin of a young buffalo bull, softly tanned, with the fur on one side, and the other finely and delicately dressed and ornamented with pictured representations of the events and battles of his life emblazoned on it by his own hand. It was worn over their shoulders (or in other words, over one shoulder and passing under the other). Often it was cut down to about half its original size to make it handy and easy for use. Many of these are also fringed on one side with scalp locks.

In all seasons a man kept this robe at hand so that he could swathe his person in it when appearing in public.

This was universally true of all except those of the plateau area and possibly some of the southern tribes. In the plateaus, the most common robes for winter were antelope, elk, and mountain sheep, while in summer elk skins without the hair were worn. Beaver skins and those of other small animals were sometimes pieced together. The Blackfoot, east of the Rocky Mountains, also used these various forms of robes. The plateau tribes sometimes used a woven blanket of strips of rabbit skin. This was also widely used in Canada and the Southwest. But this type of blanket has not been reported for the plains tribes east of the mountains.

Generally there were no differences between the robes of men and women except in their decorations. The buffalo robes were usually the entire skins with the tail. Among most tribes, the robe was worn horizontally with the tail on the right hand side. Light, durable, and gaily colored blankets were later introduced by traders.

TUNICS

The tunic or shirt for men was commonly made of two skins of deer or mountain sheep and were strung with scalp locks, beads, and ermine.

This shirt was made of two skins of the mountain sheep, artfully dressed, and sewed together by seams which rested upon the arms; one skin hung in front, over the breast, and the other fell down over the back, the head passing between them. Across each shoulder—somewhat in the form of an epaulette—was a decorative band.

This shirt itself, stripped of its ornaments and accessories, seems to be the pattern worn in daily routine. The Cree, Dene, and other tribes of central Canada wore leather shirts, no doubt because of the severe winters.

BELTS AND BREECHCLOUT

The belt, which was of a substantial piece of buckskin, was firmly wrapped and tied around his waist. In it he carried his tomahawk and scalping knife.

The breechclout was a broad strip of cloth drawn up between the legs and passed under the belt both in front and behind, ending in a small apron.

In their ordinary day-to-day life, the men of the plains were not elaborately clothed. At home, they usually went about in breechclout and moccasins.

LEGGINGS

The leggings are made of deerskins, wrapped and fitted around the leg; some were embroidered with porcupine quills passing down the seam on the outer part of the leg, and some were fringed with the scalp locks of their enemies.

They extended from the feet to the hips and were fastened to a belt that was passed around the waist.

Almost everywhere the men wore long leggings tied to the belt. But women's leggings tended to be shorter, extending from the ankle to the knee and supported by garters.

WOMEN'S WEAR

Native American women tended to wear more clothing than the men. The most typical garment was the sleeveless dress, a one-piece garment, but in some tribes—the Cheyenne, Osage, and Pawnee for example—women wore a two-piece garment consisting of a skirt and a cape. This was also a form of dress typical of the woodland peoples of the East.

MOCCASINS

Their moccasins were most often made of buckskin, were ornamented with porcupine quills, and were worn by all, except for the sandals worn in the Southwest and in Mexico.

The two general structural types of moccasins in North America are the one-piece, or soft-soled moccasin, and the two-piece, or hard-soled.

The one-piece might generally be considered as a woodlands moccasin and was worn all the year round.

The two-piece had a harder sole, with an added ankle flap, which gave it a boot-like quality.

Making a One-Piece Moccasin

That part of the pattern marked "a" forms the upper side of the moccasin; "b" the sole; "e" the tongue; and "f" the trailer.

The leather is folded lengthwise, along the dotted line, the points "c" and "d" are brought together, and the edges are sewed along to the point "g," which makes a seam the whole length of the foot and around the toes.

 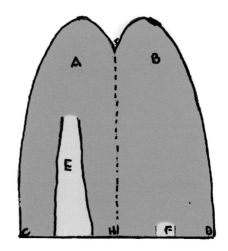

The vertical heel seam is formed by sewing "c" and "d" now joined to "h," with "f" projecting. The strips "c" and "d" are each half the width of that marked "h"; consequently the side seam at the heel is half way between the top of the moccasin and the sole, but it reaches the level at the toes. As the sides of this moccasin are not high enough for the wearer's comfort, an extension or ankle flap is sewed on, varying from two to six inches in width, cut long enough to overlap in front, and it is held in place by means of the usual draw string or lacing around the ankle.

The upper is made of soft tanned skin, and after finishing and decorating is sewed to a rawhide sole cut to fit the foot of the wearer. A top, or vamp, may be added.

Two-Piece Moccasin

On the plains the two-piece moccasin prevailed. The soles are of stiff rawhide. They conform generally to the outlines of the foot. An ankle flap is added—that is the second piece—and sometimes the tongue is separate.

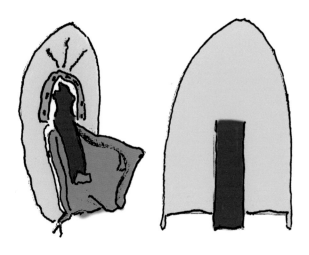

HEADWEAR

There was no universal head covering for all Native peoples. In winter the Blackfoot, Plains-Cree, and others in the north often wore fur caps. In the South, both in the East and in the West, and on the Northwest Coast, men and women turbaned their heads in fabric. In the South and on the plateaus, the eyes were sometimes protected by simple shades of rawhide. But in general, both sexes on the plains went bare headed, though the robe was often pulled up to form a kind of temporary hood.

For the peoples of the plains, the headdress—or what Europeans were to come to call "bonnets"— were of varying sorts, and many of them were exceedingly handsome; they were generally made of some combination of eagle or raven quills and of ermine. These tended to be the most costly part of an Indian's wardrobe.

These headdresses—which were superb and truly magnificent—often consisted of a crest of war eagles' quills, gracefully falling back from the forehead over the back part of the head, sometimes extending all the way down to the feet, set off in a profusion of ermine, and capped off on the top of the head with the horns of the buffalo, shaved thin and highly polished.

This headdress with horns was worn only on special occasions, and then only by men of recognized stature among the people.

HAIR DRESSING

Many of the plains tribes wore their hair uncut. Among the northern tribes, men frequently gathered the hair in two braids, but in the plateau area and among some of the southern tribes, both sexes usually wore it loose on the shoulders and back. Native American peoples throughout the eastern regions wore a *roach,* or finely worked and highly decorated pad—usually of leather—braided into their hair, glued to the scalp, or

otherwise attached to the head. The Crow men sometimes cropped the fore-lock and trained it to stand erect. The Blackfoot, Assiniboine, Yankton-Dakota, Hidatsa, Mandan, Arikara, and Kiowa trained a fore-lock to hang down over the nose. Early writers report the common practice of artificially lengthening men's hair by adding on extra strands, sometimes until it draped to the ground.

The hair of women throughout the plains was usually worn in a two-braid fashion, with the median parted from the forehead to the neck. Old women frequently allowed the hair to hang down at the sides or confined it by a simple headband. Women were fond of tracing the part line with vermilion. There was some tattooing, but noses were seldom pierced. The ears, on the other hand, were usually perforated and adorned with pendants.

Instead of combs, brushes made from the tails of porcupines were often used in dressing the hair. Ordinarily, they were made by stretching the porcupine tail over a stick of wood. The hair of the face and other parts of the body was pulled out by small tweezers.

The Oto, Osage, Pawnee, Omaha, and many Eastern peoples closely cropped the sides of the head, leaving a ridge or tuft across the crown and down behind.

Striking feather bonnets with long tails were exceptional and permitted only to a few distinguished men. They were most characteristic of the Dakota. Even a common eagle feather in the hair of a Dakota had some military significance according to its shape and position. On the other hand, objects tied in a Blackfoot's hair were almost certain to have a charm value. So far as we know, among all of the plains tribes, objects placed in the hair of men usually had more than a mere aesthetic significance.

WAR SHIELD

A war shield was made of the hide of the buffalo's neck and was hardened with the glue made from its hoofs. Its boss was sometimes fashioned from the skin of a pole-cat, its edges fringed with rows of eagles' quills and antelope hoofs.

ORNAMENT

Beads for the neck, ear ornaments, gorgets, necklaces of claws, scarves of otter, and other fur were often used. The face and exposed parts of the body were sometimes painted and often the hair as well.

TATTOOS

Tattooing was much practiced by the Native peoples of North America. Some took the form of spots on the forehead, stripes on the cheeks and chin, or rings on the arms and wrists; often the whole of the breast as low down as the navel, with both arms, was covered with drawings in tattoo.

Among the men it was often a mark of rank, distinguishing the warrior. It was usually done on females at the age of twelve to fourteen years and was often a simple design, such as a round spot in the middle of the forehead, stripes from the corners and middle of the mouth down to the chin, occasionally transversely over the cheek, and rings around the wrist and upper parts of the arms.

Men were often entirely tattooed after having faced their first enemy.

Tattooing

The material employed and the techniques were as follows:

Red willow and cedar wood were burned to charcoal, pulverized, and mixed with a little water. This provided the blue coloring ink. From four to six porcupine quills or needles were tied together with sinew. These were enveloped in split feathers and wrapped with sinew, until a stiff pencil about the size of a goose quill was had, with the quills or needles projecting at the end. One of the priests or divining men was then requested to operate. At the same time a feast of dried berries was prepared, and a considerable number of elderly men were invited to drum and sing. When all

were assembled the feast was eaten with much solemnity and invocations to the spirits.

The person to be tattooed was then placed on his back, being stripped naked, and the operator was informed of the extent of the design to be represented. He then proceeded to mark an outline with the ink, which, if correct, was punctured with the instrument above alluded to, so as to draw blood, filling up the punctures with the coloring matter as he went along by dipping the needles therein and applying them. The drumming and singing was kept up throughout the operation, which, with occasional stops to smoke, eat, or sleep, occupied from two to two and a half days.

MEDICINE BAG AND TOBACCO SACK

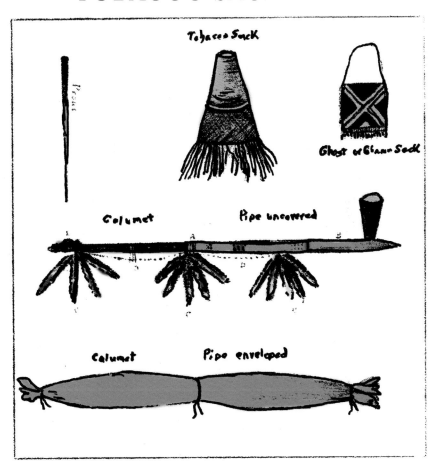

Tobacco Sack

Ghost or Charm Sack

Calumet   Pipe uncovered

Calumet   Pipe enveloped

A medicine bag was often the skin of a beaver, ornamented with hawks' bills and ermine.

A man's tobacco sack was made of the waterproof skin of an otter and decorated with porcupine quills. In it he carried his tobacco and/or *k'nick-k'neck* (the bark of the red willow, which is smoked as a substitute for tobacco). It also contained tools for fire-making and punk for lighting.

The artist George Catlin described one pipe like this:

"His Pipe, which was ingeniously carved out of the red steatite (or pipe-stone), the stem of which might be three feet long and two inches wide, made from the stalk of the young ash; about half its length was wound with delicate braids of the porcupine's quills, so ingeniously wrought as to represent figures of men and animals upon it. It was also ornamented with the skins and beaks of wood-peckers' heads, and the hair of the white buffalo's tail. The lower half of the stem was painted red, and on its edges it bore the notches he had recorded for the snows (or years) of his life."

CHAPTER NINE: GAMES AND SPORT

The sports of Native American peoples were much like the games of people everywhere, and consisted of contests of strength, agility, and cunning. They wrestled, they raced, they danced. Many games were of the simple domestic variety, suited to family life in the lodge; others involved the whole community in trials with the spear, the bow and arrow, the hatchet, and the ball.

THE HAND GAME

The hand game was a favorite gambling game. One player holds a marked and an unmarked bone in each hand, which he rapidly switches from one to the other. His opponents bet on which hand held the unmarked bone.

MOCCASIN PLAY

This can be played by two or three and is a sort of shell game, except that the pebble or other small object to be hidden is deftly transferred between three moccasins. It is a game of observation and of chance, and often the play becomes so deeply interesting that a player will stake first his gun; next his steel traps; then his implements of war; then his clothing; and lastly, his tobacco and pipe, leaving him, the Ojibways say, "*Nah-bah-wan-yah-ze-yaid*," or with only a piece of cloth and a string around his waist.

TOSSING PLAY

Tossing play is a game played indoors. Several cedar boughs are tightly braided into an oblong knot of roughly seven inches. To this is attached a thin line about fifteen inches long. An oblong knot, made of cedar boughs about seven inches long, is used. On the top a string about fifteen inches long is fastened, by which the knot is swung. On the other end of this string is another stick, two and a half inches long and sharply pointed. This is held in the hand, and if the player can hit the large stick every time it falls on the sharp one, he wins.

BONE PLAY

This is another in-door amusement, so called because the articles used are made of the hoof-joint deer bone. The ends are hollowed out, and then several are strung together. In playing it they use the same kind of sharp stick, the end of which is thrown into the hollows of the bones.

THE ARROW GAME

The arrow game is a contest favored by peoples of the prairies, generally those who employ the short bow. The contestants assemble a short distance from the village. Each entrant "puts up" his ante in order to compete. This might be a robe, a shield, a pipe, etc. Then each step forward in turn, shooting his arrows into the air. The aim is to see who can get the greatest number of arrows, from the same bow, flying at one time. The trick is to elevate the first arrow so that it is airborne for the longest time possible, and while it is flying, the others are discharged as rapidly as possible. He who succeeds in getting the most arrows in the air at one time is the winner and is awarded the goods staked.

RING AND STICK

There are many variations of this game, but essentially it is a contest played outdoors on a hard flat surface. Generally two champions are named, and they alternately choose others until they have formed two teams. Next the members of the community place bets on their favorites. These "stakes" are held by elders who also referee the match. At the start of each round two players—one from each team—trot abreast of one another, armed with a six-foot-long stick (the Mandan people called this stick *tchung-kee*) with little strips of inch-long leather projecting from its sides. Ahead of them another player rolls a small stone ring. The aim of the game is to throw or slide the stick into the ring. The number of points is awarded depending on the position of the leather strips touching the inside of the ring in which the stick has lodged. The winner of each round rolls the ring in the following round.

HOOP AND POLE

This is another variation of the ring and stick game, except in this case the ring is a hoop of braided twigs,

inner-meshed with leather thongs, that is tossed into the air; the players throw long slender poles—their front ends split and reinforced to resemble claws. The aim is to "capture" the hoop.

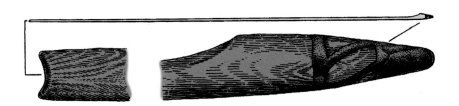

SNOWSNAKE

Snowsnake was played in wintertime, most commonly by eastern woodland peoples. A long meandering trough was cut through the snow, often across a broad hillside. The snowsnake itself was a long, thin, hardwood stick about the length of a man, rubbed with ocher, smooth, and well greased with fat or beeswax. The tail or back end of the "snake" was notched for the player's index finger. The nose or front was carved to resemble the head of a snake and was somewhat thicker than the tail.

Sometimes this head was of carved stone, embedded into the stick. After the Europeans came, this head was often fashioned of lead. The idea was to make the front end heavier and thus increase its propulsion. The game was played in turns, and each contestant ran and launched his snowsnake down the trench. Whoever's "snake" went farthest was the winner.

BALL PLAY

In the early 1830s, the painter George Catlin traveled in the southeastern territories, among the Choctaw peoples. Later he would describe their "ball-play," which we know as lacrosse.

Whilst I was staying at the Choctaw agency in the midst of their nation, it seemed to be a season of amusements, a kind of holiday; when the whole tribe, almost, were assembled around the establishment, and from day to day we were entertained with many games or feats that were exceedingly amusing: horse-racing, dancing, wrestling, foot-racing, and ball-playing were amongst the most exciting; and of all the catalogue, the most beautiful was decidedly that of ball-playing. This wonderful game is the favorite one among all the tribes.

It is no uncommon occurrence for six or eight hundred or a thousand of these young men to engage in a game of ball, with five or six times that number of spectators, of men, women, and children, surrounding the ground and looking on. And I pronounce such a scene, with its hundreds of Nature's most beautiful models, denuded and painted of various colors, running and leaping into the air, in all the most extravagant and varied forms in the desperate struggles for the ball.

I have made it a uniform rule, whilst in the Indian country, to attend every ball-play I could hear of, if I could do it by riding a distance of twenty or thirty miles; and on such occasions my usual custom has been to straddle the back of my horse and look on to the best advantage. In this way I have sat, and oftentimes reclined, and almost dropped from my horse's back, with irresistible laughter at the succession of droll tricks, kicks, and scuffles that ensue, in the almost superhuman struggles for the ball.

These plays generally commence at nine o'clock, or near it, in the morning; and I have more than once balanced myself on my pony, from that time till near sundown, without more than one minute of intermission at a time, before the game has been decided.

One Monday afternoon at three o'clock, I rode out to a very pretty prairie, about six miles distant, to the ball-play-ground of the Choctaws, where we found several thousand Indians encamped. There were two points of timber about half a mile apart, in which the two parties for the play, with their respective families and friends, were encamped; and lying between them, the prairie on which the game was to be played. My companions and myself, although we had been apprised that to see the whole of a ball-play we must remain on the ground all the night previous, had brought nothing to sleep upon, resolving to keep our eyes open and see what transpired through the night. During the afternoon, we loitered about amongst the tents of the two encampments, and afterwards, at sundown, witnessed the ceremony of measuring out the ground and erecting the "byes" or goals, which were to guide the play.

Each party had their goal made with two upright posts, about twenty-five feet high and six feet apart, set firm in the ground, with a pole across at the top. These goals were about forty or fifty rods apart; and at a point just halfway between, there was another small stake, driven down, where the ball was to be thrown up at the firing of a gun to be struggled for by the players. All this preparation was made by some old men who were selected to be the judges of the play, who drew a line from one bye to the other; on both sides gathered a great concourse of women and old men, boys and girls, and dogs and horses, where bets were to be made on the play. The betting was all done across this line and seemed to be chiefly left to the women, who seemed to have marshaled out a little of everything that their houses and their fields possessed: goods and chattels—knives—dresses—blankets—pots and kettles—dogs and horses, and guns.

The sticks with which this tribe play are bent into an oblong hoop at the end, with a sort of slight web

of small thongs tied across to prevent the ball from passing through. The players hold one of these in each hand, and by leaping into the air, they catch the ball between the two nettings and throw it, without being allowed to strike it or touch it in their hands.

In every ball play of these people, it is a rule of the play that no man shall wear moccasins on his feet or any other dress than his breechclout around his waist, with a beautiful bead belt and a "tail" made of white horsehair or quills.

This game had been arranged and "made up" three or four months before the parties met to play it, in the following manner:

The two champions who led the two parties, and had the alternate choosing of the players through the whole tribe, sent runners with the ball-sticks most fantastically ornamented with ribbons and red paint to be touched by each one of the chosen players; who thereby agreed to be on the spot at the appointed time and ready for the play. The ground having been all prepared and preliminaries of the game all settled, and the bets all made, and goods all "staked," night came on without the appearance of any players on the ground. But soon after dark, a procession of lighted flambeaux was seen coming from each encampment to the ground where the players assembled around their respective byes; and at the beat of the drums and chants of the women, each party of players commenced the "ball-play dance" party and danced for a quarter of an hour around their respective byes in their ball-play dress; rattling their ball-sticks together in the most violent manner, and all singing as loud as they could raise their voices; whilst the women of each party, who had their goods at stake, formed into two rows on the line between the two parties of players and danced also, in a uniform step, and all their voices joined in chants to the Great Spirit, in which they were soliciting his favor in deciding the game to their advantage and also encouraging the players to exert every power they possessed in the struggle that was to ensue.

In the meantime, four old medicine men, who were to have the starting of the ball and who were to be judges of the play, were seated at the point where the ball was to be started and busily smoking to the Great Spirit for their success in judging rightly, and impartially, between the parties in so important an affair.

This dance was one of the most picturesque scenes imaginable, and it was repeated at intervals of every half hour during the night and exactly in the same manner; so that the players were certainly awake all the night and arranged in their appropriate dress, prepared for the play which was to commence at nine o'clock the next morning. In the morning, at the hour, the two parties and all their friends

were drawn out and over the ground. At length the game commenced with the judges throwing up the ball at the firing of a gun; an instant struggle ensued between the players, who were some six or seven hundred in numbers. All were mutually endeavoring to catch the ball in their sticks and throw it home and between their respective stakes.

In this game every player was dressed alike, that is, divested of all dress except the girdle and the tail; and in these desperate struggles for the ball, where hundreds are running together and leaping, actually over each other's heads and darting between their adversaries' legs, tripping and throwing and fouling each other in every possible manner, every voice was raised to the highest key in shrill yelps and barks. There are rapid successions of feats, and of incidents, that astonish and amuse far beyond the conception of anyone who has not had the singular good luck to witness them. In these struggles, every mode is used that can be devised to oppose the progress of the foremost who is likely to get the ball; and these obstructions often meet desperate individual resistance, which terminates in a violent scuffle and sometimes in fisticuffs when their sticks are dropped, and the parties are unmolested whilst they are settling it between themselves—unless it be by a general stampede.

Every weapon, by a rule of all ball-plays, is laid by in their respective encampments, and no man is allowed to go for one; so the sudden broils that take place on the ground are suddenly settled without any probability of much personal injury, and no one is allowed to interfere in any way with the contentious individuals.

There are times when the ball gets to the ground and such a confused mass rushes together around it, knocking their sticks together without the possibility of any one getting or seeing it for the dust that they raise, then the condensed mass of ball-sticks, shins, and bloody noses moves around the different parts of the ground, sometimes for a quarter of an hour at a time, without any one of the mass being able to see the ball which they are scuffling for.

Each time the ball is passed between the stakes of either party, one is counted for their game, and a halt of about one minute is called. Then play is again started by the judges, and a similar struggle ensues; and so on until the successful party arrives at one hundred, which is the limit of the game.

MAIDEN'S BALL PLAY

Doubtless the most interesting of all games is the *Maiden's Ball Play*, in the Ojibway language, *Pah-pah'Se-Kah-way*.

The majority of those who take part in this play are young damsels, though married women are not excluded. The ball is made of two deer-skin bags, each about five inches long and one in diameter. These are so fastened together as to be at a distance of seven inches each from the other. It is thrown with a stick five feet long.

This play is practiced in summer beneath the shade of wide-spreading trees. The women of the village decorate themselves for the day by painting their cheeks with vermillion and disrobe themselves of as much unnecessary clothing as possible, braiding their hair with colored feathers which hang profusely down to the feet.

At the set time the whole village assembles, and the young men, whose loved ones are seen in the crowd, twist and turn to send sly glances to them and receive their bright smiles in return.

The same confusion exists as in the game of ball played by the men. Crowds rush to a given point as the ball is sent flying through the air. None stop to narrate the accidents that befall them, though they tumble about to their no little discomfiture; they rise making a loud noise, something between a laugh and a cry, some limping behind the others, as the women shout. Worked garters, moccasins, leggings, and vermillion are generally the articles at stake. Sometimes the Chief of the village sends a parcel before they commence, the contents of which are to be distributed among the maidens when the play is over.

CHAPTER TEN: SONG AND DANCE

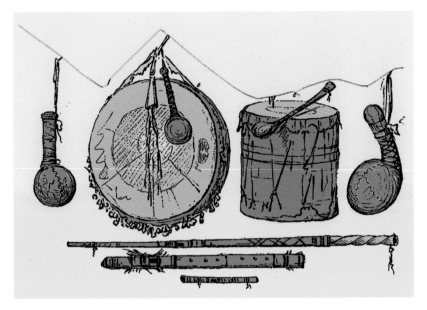

Song and dance were a vital part of life for all Native American people. No important act was performed without singing and dancing. When they wished to make war, they met to sing and dance. When they wished to beg the Great Spirit for a plentiful harvest or a good hunt, they sang and danced.

Every dance had its peculiar step, and every step had its meaning; every dance also had its peculiar song, sometimes so intricate and mysterious that few of the young men who were dancing and singing it knew the meaning of the song.

They had other dances and songs which were not so mysterious, but which were sung and understood by every person in the tribe, sung in their own language, with much poetry in them, and perfectly metered but without rhyme.

BEAR DANCE

The bear dance is performed several days in succession before starting out on the hunt, in which the hunters all join in a song to the Bear Spirit, which must be consulted and conciliated if they hope to have any success. One of the chief medicine men dons an entire skin of a bear, and with a war eagle's feather in his hand, takes the lead in the dance. The others join in singing and dancing, mimicking various attitudes and movements of the animal.

BUFFALO DANCE

The purpose here was to "make the buffalo come." These dances often continued in the village for two or three weeks, without stopping, until the herds appeared. Each hunter kept a buffalo-head mask in his lodge. This mask was worn over the head and had a strip of the animal's skin and tail attached. As the dance proceeded, when one of the dancers became tired he bent himself forward and sunk to the ground, at which

point another dancer shot him with a blunt arrow. The bystanders then dragged him by his heels out of the circle of the dance and brandished their knives around him—as though they were cutting and skinning him. Then another dancer took his place in the ceremony.

GREEN CORN DANCE

This was a dance of thanksgiving to the Great Spirit and was performed just as the corn was judged by the elders to have ripened. On that day the people are assembled and a kettle is hung over a fire and boiled. While this first kettleful is boiling, four medicine men, a stalk of the corn in one hand and a rattle in the other, with their bodies painted with white clay, dance around the kettle chanting a song of thanksgiving to the Great Spirit to whom the offering is to be made. At the same time a number of warriors dance around in a more extended circle, with stalks of the corn in their hands, joining in the song of thanksgiving while the assembled villagers look on. During this, an arrangement of wooden bowls is laid upon the ground. The dance continues until the elders judge the corn is sufficiently cooked. At this point the dance stops for a moment, while the elders place the ears on a little scaffold of sticks in the fire. Then the dance begins again, assuming a different form and song. When the corn is completely burned, it is removed from the fire and buried. Then a new fire is kindled, the corn for the feast is boiled, and all eat their fill.

SNOWSHOE DANCE

This was a dance and song performed in snowshoes just after the first snowfall, in thanksgiving to the Great Spirit for the return of snow.

DISCOVERY DANCE

This was a great favorite, and less a religious dance than a funny, popular one. It was performed without music or song or any sound except the simultaneous patting of feet. As it proceeded, one or more dancers in turn would halt and point as though pretending to see the coming of enemies or game.

BEGGAR'S DANCE

In this dance everyone sang as loud as they were able, uniting their voices in an appeal to the Great Spirit to

open the hearts of the people to give to the poor and in need, assuring them that the Great Spirit will be kind to those who aid the needy and helpless.

TRADITIONAL ALGONQUIN WAR SONG

War Song

At the start, the warrior fixes his eyes on the sky.

O shá wan ong	From the south
Un dos' e wug	They come
Un dos' e wug	They come
Pe nä' se wug	Those warlike birds
Ka baim wai wá dung-ig	Hear sounds of screams on the air

The idea of ravenous birds hovering in the sky prevails.

Tod ot' to be	I will change myself to be
Tod ot' to be	I will change myself to be

Pe nä' se	A bird
Ka dow' we á we yun'	His swift body—to be like him

The warrior now rises above all fear within him.

Ne wä be na	I throw it away
Né ow a	My body
Ne wá be na	This my boast
Ne wá be na	This my boast
Né ow a	of personal bravery

He begs the Great Spirit for extraordinary power.

Na bun á kum ig	On the front part of the earth
Tshe bá be wish' em ug	First strikes the light
In do main' em ik	Such strength to me
Mon' e do	My God
Shä wa nem id	In your mercy give!

He challenges those of his people who are slow to fight.

Wä go nain, e win?	Why do you warriors
A be yun ah	Hold back
Wä wos is se, we yun	You who are marked

He declares his full purpose to enter into the war.

Ne má je, e yeh!	I go to the spot—the war path!
Ne má je, e yeh!	Repeats.
Ne me kun ah, e yeh!	My war path!
Ge zhig neen wá tin	My sky is fair and clear or "I feel Lucky"
Hoh! Ne monedo netaibuätum o win	Let others linger. Onward!

THE MAGICIAN OF LAKE HURON: AN OTTAWA TALE

At the time that the Ottowas inhabited the Mana-toline Islands in Lake Huron, there was a famous magician living amongst them whose name was Mass-wäwëinini, or the Living Statue. It happened, by the fortune of war, that the Ottowa tribe were driven off that chain of islands by the Iroquois and were obliged to flee away to the country lying between Lake Superior and the Upper Mississippi, to the banks of a lake which is still called, by the French and in memory of this migration, Lac Courtorielle, or the lake of the Cut-ears, a term which is their nom de guerre for this tribe. But the magician Masswäwëinini remained behind on the wide-stretching and picturesque Mana-toulins, a group of islands that had been deemed, from the earliest times, a favorite residence of the *manitoes* or spirits. His object was to act as a sentinel to his countrymen and keep a close watch on their enemies, the Iroquois, that he might give timely information of their movements. He had with him two boys; with their aid he paddled stealthily around the shores, kept himself secreted in nooks and bays, hauled up his canoe every night into thick woods, and carefully obliterated his tracks upon the sand.

One day he rose very early and started on a hunting excursion, leaving the boys asleep, and limiting himself to the thick woods lest he should be discovered. At length he came unexpectedly to the borders of an extensive open plain. After gazing around him and seeing no one, he directed his steps across it, intending to strike the opposite side of it; while traveling, he discovered a man of small stature who appeared suddenly on the plain before him, and advanced to meet him. He wore a red feather on his head, and coming up with a familiar air, accosted Masswäwëinini by name, and said gaily, "Where are you going?"

He then took out his smoking apparatus and invited him to smoke. "Tell me," he said, while thus engaged, "wherein does your strength lie?"

"My strength," answered Masswäwëinini, "is similar to the human race, and common to the strength given to them, and no stronger."

"We must wrestle," said the man of the red feather. "If you should make me fall, you will say to me, 'I have thrown you, *Wa ge me na.*'"

As soon as they had finished smoking and put up their pipe, the wrestling began. For a long time the strife was doubtful. The strength of Masswäwëinini was every moment growing fainter. The man of the red feather, though small of stature, proved himself very active, but at length he was foiled and thrown to the ground.

Immediately his adversary cried out, "I have thrown you: *wa ge me na*," and in an instant his antagonist had vanished. On looking to the spot where he had fallen, he discovered a crooked ear of mondamin, or Indian corn, lying on the ground, with the usual red hairy tassel at the top. While he was gazing at this strange sight and wondering what it could mean, a voice addressed him from the ground.

"Now," said the speaking ear, for the voice came from it, "divest myself of my covering—leave nothing to hide my body from your eyes. You must then separate me into parts, pulling off my body from the spine upon which I grow. Throw me into different parts of the plain. Then break my spine and scatter it in small pieces near the edge of the woods, and return to visit the place, after one moon."

Masswäwëinini obeyed these directions and immediately set out on his return to his lodge. On the way he killed a deer, and on reaching his canoe, he found the boys still asleep. He awoke them and told them to cook his venison, but he carefully concealed from them his adventure. At the expiration of the moon he again, alone, visited his wrestling ground, and to his surprise, found the plain filled with the spikes and blades of new-grown corn. In the place where he had thrown the pieces of cob, he found pumpkin vines growing in great luxuriance. He concealed this discovery carefully from the young lads, and after his return busied himself as usual in watching the movements of his enemies along the coasts of the island. This he continued till summer drew near its close. He then directed his canoe to the coast of that part of the island where he had wrestled with the Red Plume, drew up his canoe, bid the lads stay by it, and again visited his wrestling ground. He found the corn in full ear and the pumpkins of an immense size. He plucked ears of corn and gathered some of the pumpkins, when a voice again addressed him from the cornfield.

"Masswäwëinini, you have conquered me. Had you not done so, your existence would have been forfeited. Victory has crowned your strength, and from henceforth you shall never be in want of my body. It will be nourishment for the human race."

Thus his ancestors received the gift of corn.

Masswäwëinini now returned to his canoe, informed the young men of his discovery, and showed them specimens. They were astonished and delighted with the novelty.

There were, in those days, many wonderful things done on these islands. One night, while Masswäwëinini was lying down, he heard voices speaking, but he still kept his head covered as if he had not heard them.

One voice said, "This is Masswäwëinini, and we must get his heart."

"In what way can we get it?" said another voice.

"You must put your hand in his mouth," replied the first voice, "and draw it out that way."

Masswäwëinini still kept quiet and did not stir. He soon felt the hand of a person thrust in his mouth. When sufficiently far in, he bit off the fingers, and thus escaped the danger. The voices then retired, and he was no further molested. On examining the fingers in the morning, it was his surprise to find in them long wampum beads, which are held in such high estimation by all peoples. He had slept, as was his custom, in the thick woods. On going out to the open shore at a very early hour, he saw a canoe at a small distance, temporarily drawn up on the beach; on coming closer, he found a man in the bow and another in the stern, each with his arms and hands extended in a fixed position. One of them had lost its fingers: it was evidently the man who had attempted to thrust his arm down his throat. They were two *Pukwud-jininees*, or fairies. But on looking closer, they were found to be transformed into statues of stone. He took these stone images on shore and set them up in the woods.

Their canoe was one of the most beautiful structures it is possible to imagine: four fathoms in length and filled with bags of treasures of every description and of the most exquisite workmanship. These bags were of different weight, according to their contents. He busied himself in quickly carrying them into the woods, together with the canoe, which he concealed in a cave.

One of the fairy images then spoke to him and said: "In this manner, the Ottowa canoes will hereafter be loaded when they pass along this coast, although your nation are driven away by their cruel enemies the Iroquois." The day now began to dawn fully when he returned to his two young companions, who were still asleep. He awoke them and exultingly bid them cook, for he had brought abundance of meat and fish, and other viands, that were the gifts of the fairies.

After this display of good fortune, he bethought him of his aged father and mother, who were in exile at the Ottowa lake. To wish, and to accomplish his wish, were but the work of an instant with Masswäwëinini.

One night as he lay awake reflecting on their condition, far away from their native fields and in exile, he resolved to visit them, and bring them back to behold and to participate in his abundance. To a common traveler, it would be a journey of twenty or thirty days, but Masswäwëinini was at their lodge before daylight. He found them asleep and took them up softly in his arms, flew away with them through the air, and brought them to his camp on the Manatolines, or Spirit's Islands. When they awoke, their astonishment was at its highest pitch and was only equaled by their delight in finding themselves in their son's lodge, in their native country, and surrounded with abundance.

Masswäwëinini went and built them a lodge near the corn and wrestling plain. He then plucked some ears of the corn, and taking some of the pumpkins, brought them to his father and mother. He then told them how he had obtained the precious gift, by wrestling with a spirit in red plumes, and that there was a great abundance of it in his fields. He also told them of the precious canoe of the fairies, loaded with sacks of the most costly and valuable articles. But one thing seemed necessary to complete the happiness of his father, which he observed by seeing him repeatedly at night looking into his smoking pouch. He comprehended his meaning in a moment.

"It is tobacco, my father, that you want. You shall also have this comfort in two days."

"But where," replied the old man, "can you get it—away from all supplies, and surrounded by your enemies?"

"My enemies," he answered, "shall supply it—I will go over to the Nadowas of the Bear totem, living at Penetanguishine."

The old man endeavored to dissuade him from the journey, knowing their bloodthirsty character, but it was in vain.

Masswäwëinini determined immediately to go. It was now winter weather and the lake was frozen over, but he set out on the ice, and although it was forty leagues, he reached Penetanguishine the same evening. The Nadowas saw him coming—they were amazed at the swiftness of his motions, and thinking him somewhat supernatural, feared him and invited him to rest in their lodges. He thanked them, saying that he preferred making a fire near the shore. In the evening they visited him and were anxious to know the object of his journey, at so inclement a season. He said it was merely to get some tobacco for his father. They immediately made a bundle of the article and gave it to him. During the night, however, they laid a plot to kill him.

Some of the old men rushed into his lodge, their leader crying out to him, "You are a dead man."

"No, I am not," said Masswäwëinini, "but you are," accompanying his words with a blow of his tomahawk, which laid the Nadowa dead at his feet. Another and another came at him, but he dispatched them in like manner, as quickly as they came, until he had killed six. He then took all the tobacco from their smoking pouches. By this time, the day began to dawn when he set out for his father's lodge, which he reached with incredible speed, and before twilight, spread out his trophies before the old man.

When spring returned, his cornfield grew up without planting or any care on his part, and thus the maize was introduced among his people and their descendants, who have ever been noted, and are at this day, for their fine crops of this grain and their industry in its cultivation. It is from their custom of trading in this article that this tribe are called Ottowas.

CHAPTER ELEVEN: WAR AND PEACE

For as far back in time that memory goes, people have warred with one another. As the peoples of North America did not organize themselves into nation states, they rarely fought set battles, where masses of warriors confronted one another on great fields of slaughter. Rather their mode of warfare tended to be what today we would call isometric, where small bands ambushed and raided their enemies, decimating whole groups and taking captives and scalps. It was relentlessly savage, and it was more or less continuous, like a low-grade fever, forever spiking. This was warfare between people rather than between countries.

Below is a drawing—copied from the robe of a Blackfoot warrior—of a series of battles, illustrating what we might regard as typical of the warfare practiced.

A BLACKFOOT WAR RECORD

Beginning at the top, we have Bear Chief

- On foot surprised by Assiniboine Indians but he escaped;
- Double Runner cut loose four horses;

- Double Runner captures a Gros Ventre boy;
- Double Runner and a companion encounter and kill two Gros Ventre, he taking a lance from one;
- Even while a boy, Double Runner picked up a war bonnet dropped by a fleeing Gros Ventre, which in the system counts as a deed;
- As a man he has two adventures with Crow Indians, taking a gun from one;
- He, as leader, met five Flathead in a pit and killed them;
- A Cree took shelter in some cherry brush in a hole, but Big Nose went in for him;
- Not completely shown, but representing a Cree killed.

PEACE

Every struggle must come to an end, at least for a time, when the war club was put away, the fire in the hearts of the young warriors dampened, and the pipe of peace was smoked.

But peace is not only the absence of war, it is also a matter of the heart, of coming to terms with loss and anger and grief. The Haudenosaunee—we call them Iroquois, but that was a name given them by their enemies—practiced (some still practice them) *Condolence* or *Rekindling* ceremonies during which strings of wampum are displayed and exchanged. There were (are) a number of versions of these rituals, but the point is to celebrate the passing of the warrior or chief, to raise up a new leader, and to bring peace to the people's hearts.

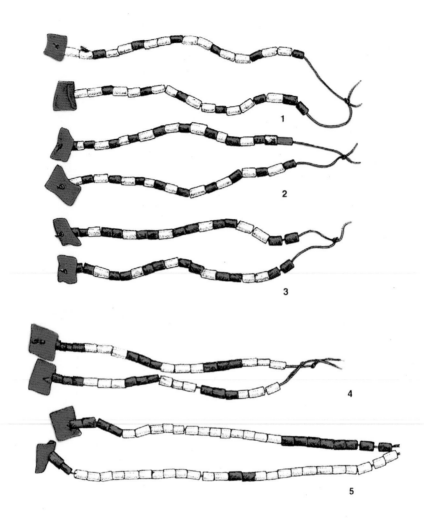

(1) The *Tears* or the *Eyes* (to wipe away the tears)
(2) The *Ears* (to clear the ears)
(3) The *Throat* (to clear the throat)
(4) *Within his Breast* (to restore the disarranged organs within the body)
(5) The *Bloody Husk Mat Bed* (to wipe the bloodstains from the mat)

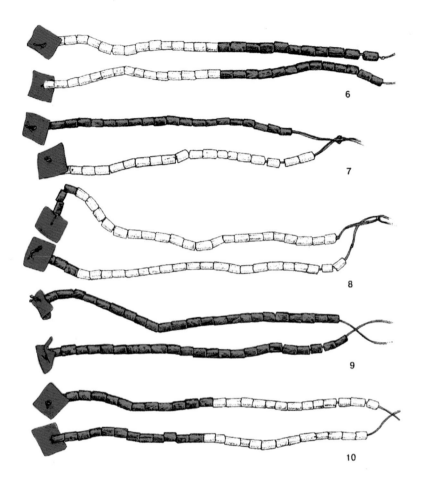

(6) The *Darkness of Grief* (to dispel the darkness and bring on the day)

(7) The *Loss of the Sky* (to cause the sky to be beautiful)

(8) The *Loss of the Sun* (to replace the sun in the sky)

(9) The *Grave Cover* (to level the earth over the grave)

(10) The *Twenty Matters* (twenty is the penalty for murder)

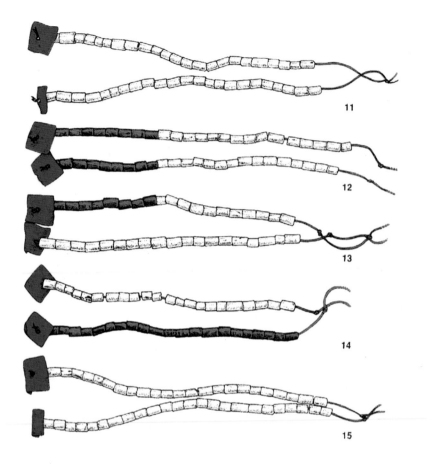

(11) The *Council Fire* (to gather the scattered
      firebrands, rekindle the fire)

(12) The *Creator's Assistants—Matron and Warrior* (to
      cheer their hearts)

(13) The *End of Insanity* (to dispel the insanity caused
      by grief)

(14) The *Torch* (to restore the torch carried through
      the longhouse announcing the death)

(15) The *Federation Chief* (to restore the chief by
      raising him up and naming him)